Shirley Shafer
3625 W. Part au Prince
Phoenix, Az 85023

BREADS
FROM MANY LANDS

Lois Lintner Sumption and
Marguerite Lintner Ashbrook

WITH PENCIL DRAWINGS BY
AMELIA REINMANN

DOVER PUBLICATIONS, INC.
NEW YORK

Published in Canada by General Publishing Company, Ltd., 30 Lesmill Road, Don Mills, Toronto, Ontario.

Published in the United Kingdom by Constable and Company, Ltd., 10 Orange Street, London WC2H 7EG.

This Dover edition, first published in 1982, is an unabridged republication of the revised (1948) edition of the work first published in 1941 by The Manual Arts Press, Peoria, Illinois, under the title *Breads and More Breads: Recipes from Many Nations.*

Manufactured in the United States of America
Dover Publications, Inc.
180 Varick Street
New York, N.Y. 10014

Library of Congress Cataloging in Publication Data

Sumption, Lois Lintner.
  Breads from many lands.

  Reprint. Originally published: Breads and more breads. Rev. ed. Peoria, Ill.: Manual Arts Press, 1948.
  Bibliography: p.
  Includes index.
  1. Bread. 2. Cookery, International. I. Ashbrook, Marguerite Lintner. II. Title.
TX769.S835 1982   641.8′15   81-19449
ISBN 0-486-24327-3 (pbk.)   AACR2

TO

ADA MORGAN LINTNER
AND
HARRY HODGE LINTNER

OUR PARENTS WHO HAVE TAUGHT US
THE JOY OF THE HOME-BAKED LOAF

AND TO ALL OTHERS
WHO HAVE SO GRACIOUSLY AIDED US

THIS BOOK
IS AFFECTIONATELY DEDICATED
BY THE AUTHORS

CONVERSION TABLES FOR FOREIGN EQUIVALENTS

DRY INGREDIENTS

Ounces	Grams	Grams	Ounces	Pounds	Kilograms	Kilograms	Pounds
1 =	28.35	1 =	0.035	1 =	0.454	1 =	2.205
2	56.70	2	0.07	2	0.91	2	4.41
3	85.05	3	0.11	3	1.36	3	6.61
4	113.40	4	0.14	4	1.81	4	8.82
5	141.75	5	0.18	5	2.27	5	11.02
6	170.10	6	0.21	6	2.72	6	13.23
7	198.45	7	0.25	7	3.18	7	15.43
8	226.80	8	0.28	8	3.63	8	17.64
9	255.15	9	0.32	9	4.08	9	19.84
10	283.50	10	0.35	10	4.54	10	22.05
11	311.85	11	0.39	11	4.99	11	24.26
12	340.20	12	0.42	12	5.44	12	26.46
13	368.55	13	0.46	13	5.90	13	28.67
14	396.90	14	0.49	14	6.35	14	30.87
15	425.25	15	0.53	15	6.81	15	33.08
16	453.60	16	0.57				

LIQUID INGREDIENTS

Liquid Ounces	Milliliters	Milliliters	Liquid Ounces	Quarts	Liters	Liters	Quarts
1 =	29.573	1 =	0.034	1 =	0.946	1 =	1.057
2	59.15	2	0.07	2	1.89	2	2.11
3	88.72	3	0.10	3	2.84	3	3.17
4	118.30	4	0.14	4	3.79	4	4.23
5	147.87	5	0.17	5	4.73	5	5.28
6	177.44	6	0.20	6	5.68	6	6.34
7	207.02	7	0.24	7	6.62	7	7.40
8	236.59	8	0.27	8	7.57	8	8.45
9	266.16	9	0.30	9	8.52	9	9.51
10	295.73	10	0.33	10	9.47	10	10.57

Gallons (American)	Liters	Liters	Gallons (American)
1 =	3.785	1 =	0.264
2	7.57	2	0.53
3	11.36	3	0.79
4	15.14	4	1.06
5	18.93	5	1.32
6	22.71	6	1.59
7	26.50	7	1.85
8	30.28	8	2.11
9	34.07	9	2.38
10	37.86	10	2.74

HISTORY

Bread, as ancient as man himself, comes to us with an interesting linguistic background as well as a history rich in color and incident. The original teutonic survives in our word "loaf," from the Old English "hlāf," that meant bread as the general substance. By 1200 the Anglo-Saxon word "bread," containing the idea of bit or piece of bread, changed places with the word "hlāf" in meaning, and bread became the general term, while loaf meant the small unit of the general substance.

The bread of our remote ancestors, as we know from calcined remains found in the Swiss Lake Dwellings, was made by grinding, with stones, sometimes called a "quern," barley or wheat into a coarse flour, mixing this with water into small, round shapes, and drying them in the sun or baking them on heated, convex stones covered with hot ashes. Sometimes the cakes were made with acorns and beechnuts for flour; this system survives today with some of the Indians on the Pacific who make a bread of crushed acorns soaked in water and squeezed dry, then shaped into a cake and dried in the sun.

The Egyptians were considered good bakers, having evolved a time-saving device for both kneading clay in the hands to make vessels and, at the same time, kneading dough with their feet. They used two kinds of flour: spelt, a good, wheat flour, and durra, made from barley. The wealthy people used the former, and it is interesting to see that the preference for white flour remained a mark of the higher classes down through history until our interest in health led people to believe that the coarser flours were better for us. That the Egyptians knew of the powers of yeast is known from remains, in tombs, of bread containing dead yeast cells. Modern Egyptian bakers are accused of knowing so much about yeast growth that their ambition is to get the biggest loaf of yeast bread from the smallest amount of dough, with the result that much of their bread resembles holes wrapped in crust.

The Greeks are said to have had over fifty kinds of bread, using such flours as wheat, barley, rye, dried lotus root, millet, spelt, and rice. Their story of the origin of leavened bread is that some slaves happened to leave some dough in the kneading trough, only to find when they returned that it was all bubbly. They put this mass with the new batch of dough, probably for reasons of economy, and found that the whole mass began to rise. That seemed like such a good idea that they passed it on to the other bakers. At that time the public bakeries, controlled by the government, were the gossip centers and the meeting places.

Rome carried on the idea of the public bakery and borrowed Greeks, who had the reputation of being the best bakers, to manage them. Running true to form in legal stipulations, Rome required that every baker stamp his loaves with some insignia. We are told by Apicius, the famous old Roman gourmet, that the bread of Picentia was the very best, and it is interesting to note in passing that he gives recipes for bread poultices that the ladies wore as complexion aids!

Individual bakers in England during the middle ages gradually grouped themselves into guilds with very strict rules for apprentices. By 1307 there were two large guilds in London, called "The Company of the White Bakers" and "The Company of the Brown Bakers." In the seventeenth century both united into one. The bakers must have been out to "gyp" the public, for we find restrictions and severe penalties imposed upon those bakers who failed to live up to the letter of the law. Here are some of the laws: White bread must be marked with "W", the household bread for the lower classes with "H", and any bread having mixed flour with "X". The innkeeper must never make his own bread. In London only farthing and ha'penny loaves could be sold, and they must be stamped. If women distributed the bread, they were given thirteen loaves, but paid for only twelve, having the extra loaf for their profit; and that is said by some to be the origin of the "baker's dozen." Others say that the Law was so strict, the bakers formed the habit of throwing an extra in, just to be sure. In the early days bakers were not allowed to sell at retail, but as a kind of heart balm they were the only class who could keep pigs in their houses. It was thought that with the pigs to eat the waste, the bakers would not be tempted to make the bread too coarse!

Trouble lay in store for any baker who tried to cheat in the time of Edward I.

If any default be found in the bread of a baker in the city, the first time let him be drawn upon a hurdle from the Guildhall to his own house through the great streets where the most people are assembled and through the great streets which are the most dirty, with the faulty loaf hanging round his neck; if a second time he shall be found committing the same offense let him be drawn from the Guildhall through the great street of Cheepe in the manner aforesaid to the pillory and there remain at least one hour in the day, and the third time that such default shall be found he shall be drawn, and the oven shall be pulled down and the baker made to foreswear the trade in the city forever.

This may sound severe, but it is tame compared to a penalty sometimes imposed, called the "Cathedra stercoralis": the culprit was tied to a chair and ducked in the contents of a cesspool!

At this time there were three general classifications of bread, with many varieties under each. Manchet or simnel was the finest type; chete was made of a coarser flour; while black bread was very coarse, the bread of the poor.

The very finest manchet was the *pain demayn,* derived from the Pains Dominicus, or the Lord's Bread, so named because on each loaf was pressed the image of the face of the Savior. Originally this bread was baked by the nuns and used for the Lord's Supper, and the unconsecrated loaves were sold to the nobility. Later, during the feudal period, when each lord had his own bake oven, the manchet was baked for the lord's table and the religious significance was dropped. Here is the way manchets were made in 1615, according to Gervaise Markham:

Your best and principal bread is Manchet, which you shall bake in this manner: First, your meal being ground upon the black stones, if it be possible, which makes the whitest flour, and passed through the finest boulting [sifting] cloth, you shall put it into a clean kimnel, and opening the flower hollow in the midst, put into it of the best ale brew the quantity of three pints to a bushel of meal and some salt to season it with; then put in your liquor reasonable warm, and knead it very well together with both your hands, and through the brake, or for want thereof, fold it in a cloth, and with your feet tread it a good space together then letting it lye an hour or thereabouts to swell, take it forth and mould it into Manchets round and flat, scotch them about the waste to give it leave to rise, and prick it with your knife in the top, and so put it into the oven and bake it with a gentle heat.

The manchet is always shaped by the hand, as the term implies, and is not put in a tin to give it shape as it rises. The term is still used in some parts of England.

Wastel bread for the prosperous, middle class was made of wheat flour but of a lower quality than that used in the manchet. French bread or puffe was next in the order of descending quality. Cocket was still less fine and always marked with a seal. Tourte, or twisted bread, was used in monasteries and for some of the poor. Trete or bis was made from white flour left after the fine parts were removed for the better bread. Chete was originally made only from unbolted rye, but it came to include all these coarser types of bread. Then, black bread was very much like the schwartz or pumpernickle of the continent today. Horse bread, as the name implies, was of very coarse flour made from peas and beans, yet it is said that horse bread was not always reserved for the horses!

The religious groups had a separate classification of breads for their use. For the abbots and important guests there was Pains Armigerorum. Pains Conventucilis was for the brethren of the order. Pains Puerorum was for the boys of the cloister school, while the servants in the monastery had Pains Famulorum.

Not only did the kind of bread indicate social standing, but the degree of freshness was important, too. Thus, freshly baked bread was for royalty; one-day-old for nobility; two-day-old for the gentry; three-day-old for scholars and friars; and four-day-old for the peasants, poor peasants!

So bread has had an interesting and vastly significant history. In time of peace, people work for it; in time of war, they fight for it. Rulers have made numerous laws regarding the use of it. At one time in England, an old law of Alexander II was revived. It was called the "Trial of Bread and Cheese." A "trial slice," consecrated by the priest, was given to one accused, who, if guilty of the crime, promptly choked. People have cried for bread, and they've romanced about it in literature. Everyone remembers Alfred and his burnt cakes; Marie Antoinette and her "let them eat cake" story; the unleavened bread of the Bible with the command, "In the sweat of thy brow shalt thou eat thy bread;" the loaf in the Rubaiyat; and Juvenal's famous saying, "Two things only the people anxiously desire, bread and the circus games." They're still at it, these people, and may this book help them to part of their desire.

INTRODUCTION

One of my favorite sports is to ask a group of my friends this question: If you were exiled to a remote island where a boat would call once a week to leave you necessary supplies, and if, while you were there, you had to live exclusively on three foods, which three would you choose?

No one has ever looked bored at the question. All brighten and begin to think, usually aloud. They name three, change their minds, revise the list, discuss, and finally make a positive statement: "I'd have to have bread." Then they add the other two favorites, and I have found that the majority settle at last on bread and butter, as one item; beef; and oranges.

Those few who preface their selections with, "I wouldn't need bread; I rarely eat it," in the end come back to bread, realizing that given only three foods, bread would be the one much-inclusive necessity.

I never think of breads that I do not remember with amusement and a sense of warm, happy comfort an experience in Holland.

We crossed, one rainy night in October, from Harwich, England, to the Hook of Holland. The Cook office had assured us a first-class cabin, and we had a first-class cabin that was, by comparison to first-class ocean travel, a kennel. It was clean and private! No more could be said for it.

The engines thumped against our thin partitions, the channel churned, the ship pitched. We were both very, very ill, and we arrived at our hotel in Amsterdam feeling like ghosts of ourselves, and as empty as ghosts.

A porter led us down a long corridor to the beautiful room assigned us. Once there, he looked at us with what doubtless was an experienced eye. "Breakfast?" he inquired, and the word seemed to imply that breakfast was what we must have, and also that he knew which breakfast we needed.

My husband looked at me, I at him. Would we ever eat again?

"Yah," said the porter firmly.

My husband wavered, then echoed, "Yah. Coffee. A good breakfast."

I heard myself feebly breathing, "Yah."

Left alone with the truly splendid bath, we made use of it, and when we were clean, rubbed, flannel-robed, there was a knock. A table entered, followed by a waiter, and before us was The Good Breakfast. We were as surprised as you will be. It consisted of a coffee service, a small silver tray of cheeses, in all the cheese hues, cut in thin, exact slices; and a silver tray of breads, in all the bread hues, cut in thin, exact slices.

There was bread almost literally black, bread brown, yellow, and white. It was the most beautiful bread I have ever seen, and that was the finest breakfast of my life, bar none.

Americans will use the recipes in this book. They are valuable because they have been adapted from original sources. I think the cooks would be wise to stick to the rules exactly, for these adaptations have not changed the breads but made the recipes easy for Americans to follow. No nation in the world could improve on time-tested Dutch bread, for instance. I hope no one will think it advisable to try.

MARJORIE BARCLAY McCLURE

Author of

High Fires
A Bush That Burned
John Dean's Journey, etc.

TABLE OF CONTENTS

MAKE THESE IF YOU HAVE

Sour Cream

Sour Milk or Buttermilk

MAYBE YOU WOULD LIKE TO TRY THESE

IF YOU ARE TO HAVE PERFECT RESULTS WITH THESE RECIPES,
IT IS IMPERATIVE THAT YOU READ
ALL OF THE INTRODUCTORY MATERIAL.

SUGGESTED EQUIPMENT

NECESSARY

1. Muffin pans

2. Baking pans in assorted shapes and sizes

3. Breadboard

4. Rolling pin

5. Spatula

6. Mixing bowls in assorted sizes

7. Rotary egg beater

8. Measuring spoons and cups in assorted sizes

9. Waffle iron

10. Heavy skillet

11. Flour sifter

SUGGESTED EQUIPMENT

NOT NECESSARY, BUT FINE TO HAVE

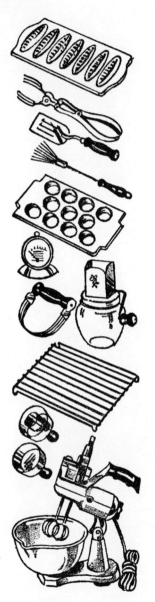

1. Corn-stick pans

2. Tweezing forks for lifting hot pans from the oven

3. Pancake turner (knives or spatula may be used)

4. Brush for greasing pans

5. Popover irons

6. Oven thermometer

7. Pastry mixer (two knives may be used)

8. Nut grinder

9. Racks for cooling loaves (four jar lids may be used)

10. Biscuit and doughnut cutters (glasses or can lids may be used)

11. Electric mixer

HOW TO USE THIS BOOK

In this book we use the word bread in its broadest sense to include loaf and small forms, both quick and yeast. Each of the recipes has been tested according to these rules, which should be followed carefully to insure perfect results:

1. Key to the symbols:

B.P. .... baking powder
B. sugar.............. brown sugar
C. sugar.............. confectioner's sugar
G. sugar .... granulated sugar
c .... cup
t .... teaspoonful
T .... tablespoonful
f.g. .... few grains

2. All measurements are level.

3. All flour is sifted once before measuring except graham, corn meal, whole-wheat, and cracked wheat. Any type of all-purpose flour may be used, but it must be remembered that different kinds and brands absorb different amounts of liquid, and, in some cases in making yeast breads, a little more flour should be added for kneading; this will not harm the product.

4. All sugar is granulated unless otherwise stated. B. sugar must be packed down in the measuring cup in order to get the amount of sweetening called for, because it has

a tendency to pack loosely. C. sugar must be sifted before measuring, to remove lumps.

5. All yeast referred to is compressed, sometimes called moist, loose, or quick. Dry yeast may be substituted according to the rules stated under the list of substitutions (p. 28).

6. All fruit and nuts are added to the sifted-together, dry ingredients, and no extra flour is needed to flour them.

7. All bar chocolate must be melted over water to prevent lumping and burning.

8. All pans are well greased with shortening other than butter, as butter makes things stick. Flouring is not necessary.

9. All loaf breads may be baked as rolls or muffins if the baking time is shortened to from one-third to one-half the time called for in baking the loaf.

10. All baking temperatures are given in the general terms—slow, moderate, and hot, because this is most practicable for all types of ovens. People who have oven thermometers and regulators may translate those terms to suit their own ovens. For your convenience we list these general rules, but see p. 29:

A. *Yeast breads in loaves* are put in a hot oven about 10 minutes to stop the growth of the yeast; then the temperature is lowered and the baking continued for about 45 minutes to bake the bread thoroughly.

B. *Yeast breads in small forms* are baked in a hot oven about 15 minutes or more depending on the size and the amount of fruit in the dough. Fruit takes longer to bake.

C. *Quick breads in loaves* are baked in a moderate oven from 45 to 60 minutes or more, depending on the size of the loaf and the amount of fruit in the dough.

D. *Quick breads in small forms* are baked in a moderate oven from 15 to 30 minutes, with the exception of waffles, pancakes, doughnuts, and biscuit that have special rules given with each recipe.

11. Steaming—Any quick bread supposed to be steamed may be baked in a slow oven instead, but the bread will have more crust. Bread may be mock steamed by baking it in covered coffee cans, with the lid slightly tilted to keep the loaf from getting too moist. Ten minutes before the baking time is over, the lid should be removed, to dry and brown the bread a little. For regular steaming, put the dough in greased, covered cans. Place them in a heavy pan half full of water. Cover tightly and steam.

12. Substitutions—Wherever possible these recipes should be made exactly as given, but sometimes it is necessary to make substitutions, if the ingredients called for are not available. This list is given only as a guide to be followed in case of necessity.

A. *Milk*

1. ½ c evaporated milk and ½ c water equals 1 c sweet milk.

2. 1 c sweet milk and 1 T vinegar equals 1 c sour milk.

3. 1 c sour milk and ½ t soda equals 1 c sweet milk, but the amount of B.P. called for in the sweet milk recipe must be used regardless of the soda.

4. Half water may be used in place of milk, but the product will not be so fine.

5. Sour milk and buttermilk may be used interchangeably, but the buttermilk makes a slightly richer product, depending on the amount of butter in it.

6. Sour cream varies so in butterfat content that it is difficult to make a rule about substituting it for milk and shortening in a recipe. In general, it may be substituted for the milk, and the shortening omitted.

B. *Flour*

1. Whole-wheat, graham, and cracked wheat flours may be used interchangeably.

2. A type of whole-wheat flour may be made by mixing ⅔ c white flour and ⅓ c cooking bran or "all bran."

3. Prepared bran cereals may be used in place of cooking or all bran, but the resulting product is always a bit soggy. These cereals should be used only in recipes especially designed for them.

4. Rye flour may be substituted for barley flour.

5. Any type of flour such as buckwheat, corn meal, or soy bean, may replace one-fourth of the flour in a recipe calling for all white flour.

C. *Shortening.* If a good, buttery flavor is important in the more delicate types of bread, use butter. Otherwise, substitute in the interests of economy, but be sure that the flavor of the shortening you use will be hidden by the flavor of the ingredients in the recipe. The bacon flavor is desired by many in corn bread, for instance, but it would be too strong for most people in date bread. Use these substitutions with discretion. Here are the equivalents of 1 c butter:

1. ⅞ c lard (1 c minus 2 T)
2. ⅞ c oleomargarine
3. ⅞ c corn, cottonseed, or nut oil (common cooking oil)
4. ⅘ c clarified drippings (bacon or combination)
5. ⅔ c clarified chicken fat
6. ⅞ c clarified fat left from deep frying if no strong-flavored articles have been fried in it.

D. *Sugar*

1. G. sugar may be substituted for B. sugar, but the flavor of the product will be changed.
2. Syrup, molasses, or honey may be substituted for sugar, but there are so many special rules to follow that we do not advise it.
3. If any of the recipes are too sweet for individual tastes, as much as ¼ the amount of sugar called for may be omitted without spoiling the recipe.

E. Corn syrup may be substituted for honey in the interests of economy, with only a slight change in flavor.

F. *Nuts*

1. If the type of nut called for is not available, any other may be used with only a slight change in flavor resulting.

2. If no nuts are available, the same amount of some substance such as coconut, Grape-Nuts, or finely chopped, dried fruit may be substituted, but the flavor, texture, and richness will be slightly changed.

G. *Dried fruits.* Special fruits give special flavors, but it is all right to use currants in place of raisins, or make other similar dried-fruit changes when needed.

H. *Candied peels.* May be used interchangeably with resulting flavor changes.

I. *Flavorings.* May be changed to suit the fancy, but remember that for the real, original product, the flavor called for should be used. If anise or caraway are not liked, use grated lemon or orange rind. Make any kind of substitution in liquid flavorings, with changes in flavor resulting.

J. *Eggs.* Vary in size. These recipes were tested with eggs weighing about 24 ounces to the dozen, U. S. Graded, Extra, Medium. One unbeaten egg measures about ¼ c. Judge your eggs according to this standard, and use more or less according to size.

K. *Chocolate.* 3 T cocoa equals 1-ounce square of chocolate.

L. *Yeast.* Dry yeast may be substituted for compressed by using the same amount, dissolving it in ¼ c lukewarm water, 1 T of the sugar to be used in the recipe, 2 T flour, and letting the mixture stand 4 hours before using. Then proceed as the recipe directs for compressed yeast.

13. Glazing—If special directions are not given in a recipe, use your choice of:

A. 1 beaten egg yolk mixed with 1 T water.

B. 1 beaten egg white mixed with 1 T water.

C. C. sugar mixed with water or cream to spreading consistency and ¼ t flavoring.

The first two may be brushed on the top before or after rising or just as the loaf comes from the oven. The last is put on the loaf when it is cold.

14. Baking Temperatures —

Very slow oven...................	250° F.
Slow oven	300° F.
Moderately slow oven............	325° F.
Moderate oven	350° F.
Moderately hot oven.............	375° F.
Hot oven	400° F.
Very hot oven...................	450°-500° F.

BREAD FACTS AND FANCIES

By following a recipe, anybody can make a good loaf of bread without knowing at all the intricate processes that are taking place. The chemistry of bread making is one of the most interesting stories of the kitchen, but there are many people who would rather not bake at all if they have to wade through a lot of material in which they are not interested. Those who want the complete story can find it well told in books that go into the technical part of it. In this book, we omit all the usual discussion of the various types of flours, since most of us don't care much about the milling of wheat, and go directly to a very simple story of bread.

Yeast and How It Works

Yeast is a collection of microscopic plant organisms that grow rapidly in a warm, moist environment, with a little food to aid them. The yeast plants in dry or compressed state are put in a liquid, with sugar for food and flour for food and thickening, in a room of ordinary temperature (70-80 degrees Fahrenheit). As they grow, they give off a gas, carbon dioxide, and alcohol. The gas bubbles working up through the thickened mixture make it rise, or become light, as we say. In the baking, the yeast plants are killed; their growth stops; the alcohol is driven off; the starch in the flour is cooked; and the result is a loaf of bread. There are three methods of accomplishing the result:

1. **Sponge.**—A sponge is a mixture of yeast, sugar, liquid, salt, and enough flour to make a thin batter. After the sponge has become bubbly and porous due to the action of the yeast in the batter, the rest of the ingredients are added and mixed well. Then this mixture is allowed to double in bulk, due again to the growth of the yeast in its favorite environment. It is kneaded down, made into shapes, put on a greased pan, allowed to double in bulk again, and then baked.

This is usually the overnight, or sometimes called the long method. It requires three or more risings: the sponge, the dough (in this stage it may rise and be kneaded several times), and the loaf.

The advantages of this method are that it takes only a small amount of yeast, and you may go about your other work during the times when the dough requires no attention. The disadvantages are that it takes a long time and it may require your attention at inconvenient times.

This is the method our grandmothers used because time and inconvenience were of no great consequence to them. They often made their own yeasts from hops, and, when they were lucky enough to get a particularly good starter (sponge) from their own brew, they saved a cup of it for the next bread making. Neighbors who didn't have a good hand with yeast or who had forgotten to save out a starter, frequently borrowed "sour dough" from their more fortunate friends. A nice, neighborly custom.

2. **Non-sponge method.**—The yeast is mixed with small amounts of lukewarm water and sugar and allowed to stand

for about ten minutes or until foamy. Then all the other ingredients are added and the same procedure followed as in the sponge method. This allows the yeast to grow rapidly before the ingredients that retard the yeast growth, such as eggs, flour, any large amount of sugar, shortening, and perhaps fruit and nuts, are added.

This is sometimes called the short method, since the first or sponge step is very much shortened and only two risings are necessary—the dough stage and the loaf stage. The advantage is that it takes less time for mixing and manipulating and thus does not keep you in the kitchen so long. The disadvantage lies in the extra expense involved in the greater amount of yeast required.

3. **Icebox method.**—The yeast is moistened with lukewarm water, and then all the other ingredients are added. The dough is mixed thoroughly with a spoon and put in the icebox, where the cold allows the yeast to grow only very slowly. Then, when the dough is taken from the icebox and shaped, the yeast grows rapidly in the warm room.

The advantages of this method are the short time required for mixing, the fact that the dough is always on hand for fresh rolls, that it requires no kneading (the great amount of shortening makes a tender roll, and the elasticity caused by kneading is not necessary). The disadvantage lies in the expense involved in the great amount of yeast and shortening required.

Definition of terms

There are certain common terms used in the making of yeast bread that should be explained:

1. **Kneading.**—This is a thorough manipulation of the dough by hand. There are mixers for this purpose, but there is no point in the casual baker having one. Kneading develops the gluten in the flour and makes the dough more elastic, thus holding the gas bubbles and allowing the loaf to rise and hold its shape. It also works air in.

2. **Kneading down.**—This is really the same process as kneading, but it comes after the dough has doubled in bulk. It is usually done at least once during the process of bread making and may be done several times if the dough has doubled in bulk and you do not have time to take care of it right away. Bread that has become too light will sour easily, so that this kneading down and letting rise again or putting in the icebox until you do have time to take care of it is a great help. The only danger lies in the possibility of working in too much flour in the kneading, thus making the bread tough. Use flour sparingly.

3. **Shaping into loaves or rolls.**—With the hands, shape a loaf or roll to one half the size you expect it to be when ready for baking. Make the top smooth by working the rough edges toward the bottom of the loaf.

4. **Mixing.**—This refers to the first mixing of ingredients with a spoon. If it is well done, less kneading of the dough is required.

5. **Covering the dough.**—This should be done with a clean cloth or waxed paper during the rising process in order to keep a crust from forming and to keep out dust. Greasing the top of the dough will accomplish the former, but has no effect on the latter.

6. **Rising.**—This refers to the action of the yeast expanding or pushing the dough up.

A. Rising time in general follows this rule: Dough made with 1 cake of yeast and 2 c of liquid will double in bulk in 3 hours. Each subsequent rising takes less time.

B. Rising may be hastened.

1. Use more yeast. This may be two to four times as much as called for. *This increases the cost, and sometimes produces too "yeasty" a flavor for some.*

2. Greater heat. The dough may be set where the temperature is 90 degrees, on a radiator or in a bowl of hot water. Sometimes this may cause other souring bacteria to develop, but usually the rising is finished and the baking started, thus killing the bacteria before they have time to do much harm.

3. If dough is not quite risen, put it in moderate instead of hot oven to let rise more while baking.

C. Slow rising is most desirable because the long process of fermentation brings out the best flavor of the products in the dough and makes a more tasty and better-textured bread.

Other interesting things to remember about yeast

1. Milk, potato water, or whey, if used as the liquid in bread, must be scalded first and then cooled to lukewarm in order to prevent souring in the bread.

2. Milk gives richness and flavor to bread.

3. Potato or whey help keep the loaf moist.

4. Sweet potato, pumpkin, or squash add moisture and color.

5. Shortening makes bread tender, but acts to retard the yeast growth.

6. Sugar is yeast food and gives flavor to the bread. It also retards yeast growth if used in large amounts.

7. Fruit, nuts, and other flavoring are in the bread for flavor. They tend to retard the growth of the yeast.

8. The only essentials for bread are liquid, flour, and yeast, and salt to make it palatable. Witness the French bread. All other ingredients add variety.

9. One fourth of the flour called for in a recipe may be replaced by such other materials as leftover cereal, potato, squash, pumpkin, or rice. This makes an excellent use for leftovers.

10. Large holes in bread are caused by too long rising.

11. Soggy bread is caused by too slow rising.

12. Sour, heavy bread is caused by too high temperature while rising.

13. Crisp crusts may be made by brushing the top of the loaf with slightly-beaten egg white 10 minutes before the baking is done. This also makes browner crusts, as does a brushing of milk, egg yolk, or cream.

14. Soft crusts may be made by brushing the top of the baked loaf with melted shortening, or, 10 minutes before baking is over, with a mixture made of 1 t cornstarch and 2 t cold water made into a paste and boiled 3 minutes with ¼ c boiling water. This not only makes the crust soft, but provides a base to which fruits and nuts will stick, and is therefore valuable in making coffee cakes.

15. White bread is easiest for the beginner to make because all the yeast processes work better in this flour than in the heavier types.

16. The number of loaves a recipe will make may roughly be determined in this way: $1\frac{1}{2}$ c liquid and $\frac{1}{4}$ to $\frac{1}{2}$ cake yeast yields one average-sized loaf.

17. Compressed yeast, if wrapped, will keep 3 or 4 days in a cool place. If it becomes slightly brown, it is still all right. If it is frozen, it may revive, but will be weaker. To test the activity of yeast, drop a bit of it in $\frac{1}{4}$ c warm water and 1 T sugar. If it bubbles in five minutes, it is all right. Small portions of a yeast cake do not keep well.

18. Dry yeast will keep much longer than compressed and is cheaper. The unused portion will keep as long as a whole cake. It should be kept in a tin box in a cool, dry place. For use in place of compressed yeast, see substitutions (p. 28). Either kind of yeast must be fresh, as dead yeast will not grow.

19. Wild yeast is the free yeast in the air. From it comes the salt rising bread that is so difficult to make but so good when made properly.

20. Other yeasts, such as potato or hop, may be made, but they are so uncertain that only experts should work with them.

QUICK BREADS

Quick breads—and there is an endless variety ranging from the health, bran types, to the lightest puff of a dainty tea biscuit—differ from yeast breads in the different leavening agents used, which work much faster than yeast. We don't intend to go into a long discussion of these and the way they work, but a few facts are interesting.

1. **Baking powder** is the commonest leavening agent used. There are many types, that work in slightly different ways, but for the purposes of this book they may be used interchangeably with good results. Old-time cooks made their own baking powder with soda and cream of tartar.

2. **Soda and acid.** This is the next most common agent. The soda, when sifted in with the dry ingredients, then dissolved in the liquid called for or in a small amount of warm water, reacts with such substances as sour milk or cream, buttermilk, molasses, B. sugar or acid fruit juices, forms a gas, carbon dioxide, and causes the material to rise.

3. **Air** beaten into eggs is a leavening agent less often used because it is not so dependable for most people.

4. **Steam** caused by heat acting on the liquid in a batter causes mixtures to puff up, as with Popovers.

How to Keep Breads (Quick and Yeast)

How to keep bread fresh

1. Remove the bread from the pan as soon as it is baked; cool in a place where the air can reach it on all sides. (A cake rack is good for this.)

2. When it is cold, place it in a clean, dry breadbox.

3. Wrap nut, fruit, or highly flavored bread in waxed paper to keep the flavor from mingling with any plain types that may be in the box.

4. Never keep stale bread with fresh bread, as the moisture in the fresh bread tends to be absorbed by the dry, stale bread.

5. If your breadbox is full, as it may be around holiday time, a covered pan or casserole makes a good substitute.

6. Breads mold quickly, especially in warm, moist weather; so watch for it and discard at once any moldy pieces; then scald the box.

How to freshen stale bread

1. Place the bread in the top of a double boiler and heat over water until the bread is warmed through. You may put the covered pan over a vegetable (not strong flavored) that is cooking in water, and this accomplishes the same thing but saves pans and heat.

2. Put the bread in a dampened, brown, paper bag. Place it in a moderate oven until the bag has dried out.

3. Plunge the bread quickly in and out of water. Put it in a moderate oven until it is dried out. This takes a great deal of care so as not to let the bread absorb too much water or become too dry in the oven.

How to use stale bread

Bread is sometimes too stale to freshen satisfactorily, but it may be used to advantage in these ways:

1. Slice and toast. This applies not only to white bread and brown, but to any of the tea breads, doughnuts, muffins, and rolls that are delicious if toasted, buttered, and served at once, for tea or breakfast.

2. Bread crumbs. If the bread is very hard it must be ground to make crumbs. Pancakes or waffles, if dried, may be treated the same way. These crumbs are good in scalloped dishes, croquettes, meat loaf, dressing, muffins, and pancakes if they are not from sweet bread. Sweet crumbs are good in cookies and puddings and on ice cream.

3. Bread pudding.

4. Fruit bread may be dampened and heated, then served with a sweet sauce, whipped cream, or both.

5. Corn and graham breads if split and toasted make excellent bases for corned-beef hash, creamed meat dishes, ham and poached eggs, Welsh rabbit and numerous others.

6. Croutons. Cut the bread (white is best) in cubes or finger lengths; butter before or after heating in the oven. These are fine with soup.

7. Croustades. These are made in a similar manner, but the bread is cut to make hollow squares, like boxes. The same things as in (5) are good on croustades.

8. French toast.

AMERICA

America, in breadmaking as in most things, has borrowed profusely from other countries, so that from other countries we find many breads we seem to have tasted before, as the dark rye from Russia, the crusty loaf from France, the kuchen from Germany, and the fruit breads from almost anywhere. In all of these there has been a simplification of method resulting from our use of electric mixers, mechanical refrigerators, electric ovens, and numerous short-cut gadgets for which we are famous. In some cases there is a slight change in ingredients, for we always have been people to use what we find at hand, to borrow ideas, change them if we like, and produce our own.

We do, however, have some things that are really our own, due to the fact that new food stuffs were developed in the new country, or due to our ability to invent. The American pancake is unique; it is our own contribution and not like the European pancake in anything but name. Some of our own characteristic breads were contributed by local conditions of the country. Nowadays, with all parts of the land so closely connected, we sometimes feel that sectional differences have disappeared. However, at least, we still think of corn bread and all its relatives of the ash, pone, hoe-cake variety as southern; of Boston brown bread as being of New England, even though we find them all over these United States.

Recently, our cooks seem to have been concentrating on the use of much that is unusual in breads. Ingredients such as pumpkin, squash, carrots, sweet potato, not to mention tomato juice and gumdrops, do their part—and a very effective one it is—in giving a distinctive character to many American breads.

It would be difficult to find any one bread we could call the characteristic American variety; after all, we are a melting pot. We find nothing incongruous in serving French brioche for breakfast, Russian rye in sandwiches for lunch, English muffins for tea, and Vienna bread for dinner. That is America. But however many varieties we may have or from wherever we may have taken them, they are all good.

Quick Breads in Loaves and Small Forms

Apricot
APRICOT GRAPE-NUTS BREAD

2 c scalded milk	½ c sugar
1 c Grape-Nuts	1 well-beaten egg
3 c flour	3 T melted shortening
4 t B.P.	¾ c finely ground apricots
½ t salt	

Pour the milk over the Grape-Nuts and let cool. Add the sifted-together, dry ingredients. Add the egg, shortening, and apricots. Put in greased loaf pans, and let stand 20 minutes. Bake in a moderate oven one hour.

This cuts better the next day, and will keep well several days. It makes good sandwiches with butter or cream cheese spread. Makes 2 medium loaves.

Mrs. Betty Goode Sprague, Cleveland, Ohio

APRICOT NUT-BRAN BREAD

½ c sugar	1 c cooked, dried apricots
2 T shortening	2 c flour
1 beaten egg	4 t B.P.
1 c sour milk	½ t soda
1 c all bran	½ t salt
½ c chopped nuts	

Cream the sugar and shortening. Add the egg and milk. Add the bran, nuts, and apricots. To measure the apricots, drain and pack solidly in a cup after they have been chopped. Beat the mixture well, and add the sifted-together, dry ingredients. Mix well. Put in a greased loaf pan, and bake 1 hour in a moderate oven.

If heavy, sour cream is used, the shortening may be omitted. Dried peaches may be used in place of apricots with an interesting change in flavor. This is an excellent tea bread and good for sandwiches.

Makes 1 large loaf.

APRICOT PEANUT BREAD

1½ c dried apricots	2½ c flour
¾ c chopped peanuts	5 t B.P.
2 T shortening	½ t salt
¾ c B. sugar	1 c milk
1 egg	

Cover the apricots with water, and cook five minutes. Drain, cool, and chop (a food chopper is best). Add the peanuts. Cream the shortening and sugar. Add the egg, and beat well. Add the sifted-together, dry ingredients alternately with the milk. Add the apricot, nut mixture. Stir. Put into a well-greased loaf pan, and bake in a moderate oven about 1 hour.

Since this bread is quite tart, it is a welcome change from the usual sweet, tea bread. A favorite of those who like peanuts. Makes 1 large loaf.

Mrs. Mary Alice Kyle, Cleveland, Ohio

Banana

BANANA NUT BREAD

¼ c shortening	1½ c flour
1 c sugar	½ t soda
2 beaten eggs	½ t salt
1½ c mashed banana	½ c chopped black walnuts

Cream the shortening and sugar. Add the eggs and bananas. Blend. Add the sifted-together, dry ingredients. Add the walnuts. Bake in a greased loaf pan in a moderately slow oven 45 minutes.

Nuts may be omitted if a less rich and flavorful bread is wanted. This loaf is quite moist, and will remain so.

Serve it for tea, plain or in small sandwiches. It does not go well with a meal because it is too rich. Makes 1 medium loaf.

Mrs. Genevieve Forsyth, Columbus, Ohio

BANANA BRAN BREAD

¼ c shortening	½ t salt
½ c sugar	½ t soda
1 well-beaten egg	½ c chopped nuts
1 c all bran	1½ c riced banana
1½ c flour	2 T water
2 t B.P.	1 t vanilla

Cream the shortening and sugar. Add the egg and bran. Add the sifted-together, dry ingredients to which the nuts have been added alternately with the banana, water mixture. Add vanilla. Blend. Put in a greased loaf pan, and let stand 30 minutes. Bake in a moderate oven 1-1¼ hours. Cool before cutting. Makes 1 large loaf.

Mrs. Mary Nichol Jones, Granville, Ohio

BANANA SOUR-CREAM BREAD

¼ c thick sour cream	1½ c flour
½ c B. sugar	2 t B.P.
1½ c mashed banana	½ t salt
1 c bran	½ t soda

Blend the first four ingredients. Add the sifted-together, dry ingredients, and mix well. Put in a greased loaf pan, and let stand 20 minutes. Bake in a moderate oven about 1 hour.

Makes 1 large loaf.

Biscuits

BISCUITS WITH VARIATIONS

Biscuits are one of the most versatile forms of hot bread in that they lend themselves so easily to numerous interesting variations. If the breadbox is empty, and hungry people must have their breakfast, make biscuits; if unexpected guests are your problem, solve it with biscuits; if your meals are lacking in variety, have biscuits in some variation. Contrary to the general opinion of the misinformed public, biscuits are not hard to make, even for young brides! Let them try this basic recipe. Having mastered that, they will hurry to try variations given here and invent more of their own.

BAKING-POWDER BISCUIT

2 c flour	4 T shortening
4 t B.P.	⅔ c milk (or other liquid)
1 t salt	

Sift together the dry ingredients. Mix the shortening very lightly in with a pastry blender, two case knives, or the finger tips. It is important to just barely blend the flour and shortening and not to pulverize it. Add the milk a bit at a time, tossing the flour-shortening mixture around with a fork, lightly, as you do so. Some flours do not absorb as much liquid as others; hence you may not require all the milk. The dough should just barely stick together so that you can lift it from the mixing bowl and roll or pat it out to about ½-inch thickness on a slightly floured board. Be careful not to use too much flour and not to work the dough too much, or the biscuit will be tough. Cut with a floured biscuit cutter, or a glass or can lid if the cutter is lacking, and bake on a slightly greased pan in a

BAKING POWDER BISCUIT

hot oven about 15 minutes. Serve while it is piping hot, with butter and whatever other spread your taste says is best.

VARIATIONS

Apple.—Add ½ t cinnamon and ½ c finely diced apples. Sprinkle the top of each biscuit with cinnamon, and put one thin apple slice on each.

Bacon.—Add ¼ c very crisp bits of fried bacon.

Bran.—Substitute ½ c bran for ½ c of the flour called for.

Butterscotch.—Use butter for the shortening. Roll the dough out in a ½-inch-thick sheet. Dot generously with butter, and sprinkle thickly with brown sugar. Roll as for jelly roll. Cut in ½-inch slices and place in a muffin tin, each hole of which is covered with 1 t B. sugar and ½ t butter. Bake these for 20-25 minutes, and remove from the tins at once. These are delicious with a salad luncheon.

Cinnamon.—Follow the above, sprinkling heavily with cinnamon before rolling.

Cheese.—Add ½ c grated, well-flavored cheese.

Candied peel.—Add ½ c finely chopped orange, lemon, or citron, or mixed candied fruit.

Corn.—Substitute ⅔ c corn meal for ⅔ c of the flour called for.

Deviled.—Roll the dough out in a sheet and cover with a paste of highly flavored, potted meat, sardine or anchovy paste, chutney or cheese spread. Roll as jelly roll. Cut in slices and bake. These are nice as a cocktail accompaniment.

Dropped.—Increase the milk to 1 c and drop from a spoon. These are more quickly made because they do not require rolling. Beginners should try these.

Fruit.—Add to the dough ½ c finely chopped, dried fruits such as currants, raisins, dates, apricots, figs.

Ginger.—Add ½ c sugar, 1 egg, 1 t grated orange rind, and 2 t ginger, and decrease the milk to ½ c. Any spice may be used in place of ginger.

Lemon.—Put small, unbaked biscuits together, sandwich fashion, with a mixture of 1½ t grated lemon rind, 4 T sugar, and enough lemon juice to make a spread. Orange juice and rind may be used for the lemon.

Maple.—Make as for **butterscotch,** using shaved maple sugar for B. sugar and maple syrup for the B. sugar in the bottom of the muffin tins. These are one of the greatest delicacies Vermont has to offer.

Orange.—Before baking, place on the top of each biscuit a small lump of sugar that has been soaked in orange juice.

Peanut butter.—Omit the shortening, and add the same amount of peanut butter.

Pinwheel.—This refers to the method of rolling out a sheet of dough, spreading it with any filling such as jam, marmalade, brown sugar, and nuts or Grape-Nuts, peanut butter, mincemeat, or dried fruit; rolling it as for jelly roll; and slicing it in ½-inch pieces and baking them on a greased pan so that they just touch each other. In our childhood parlance, pinwheel biscuits were always called "whirligigs."

Rye.—Substitute ½ c rye flour for ½ c of the flour called for.

Soda.—Use buttermilk or sour milk for the milk; use only 2 t B.P. and ½ t soda to neutralize the acid in the milk. These are most tender, a great delicacy especially in rural sections, but you must use a light hand on the soda or they will be dreadful!

Sweet potato.—Substitute 1 c mashed, cooked sweet potato for 1 c flour and use only about 6 T milk. Add 2 T B. sugar if you want a sweeter biscuit.

Surprise biscuit.—These are made by rolling a thin layer of dough around a date, pitted and stuffed with a pecan. Glaze the surface of each surprise with egg white slightly beaten. You'll be considered quite a cook when you serve these. The same method may be used with other "surprises," such as tiny sausages, orange sections, apple quarters, or figs; but with any other than dried fruit you will have a moist interior.

Tea biscuit.—Add 2 T sugar, 1 egg, reduce the milk to ½ c, and use 1 more T shortening.

Thimble.—Cut the biscuits in thimble size and very thin. These are fussy to make, but different.

Whole-wheat.—Use whole-wheat flour in place of the white flour. These will be rather thin and flat, but with an excellent flavor. Try them with the Thanksgiving dinner as a change from rolls, for they are excellent with turkey or other fowl.

Makes eight 2½" biscuit or fifty 1".

MARYLAND BISCUIT (Beaten)

2 c flour	2 T lard
1 t salt	5 T and 1 t water

Cut the lard into the dry ingredients, add the water gradually, and work the mass into a dough. Knead, and knead, and knead it again. Slap it and beat it with a rolling pin or a wooden potato masher. Though this sounds like heresy in biscuit making, it is necessary for the beaten biscuit because with each beating you are putting air into the dough, and the air is the only thing that will make these biscuits rise. So follow the rules of the old southern mammies and "Tak' yo' time, honey chile." Slap it and beat it and slap it some more—no matter if you do wake the white folks upstairs; they ought to be getting an appetite for breakfast anyway. Those who don't want to bother with the beating and slapping can take a short cut by putting the dough through a food chopper four or five times or until the dough feels elastic. After about twenty minutes, when you can stretch the dough out like a ribbon and it makes a snapping sound if you pull it, you can stop your hard work. With the hands, make tiny dough balls, or roll the dough out 1/4 inch thick, cut into 1-inch rounds, prick tops with a fork, and bake on a greased pan in a moderate oven, gradually increasing the heat until the biscuits are a delicate brown. This will take 45-60 minutes.

Then you'll have a crisp, flaky biscuit, like no other you ever tasted. Be very delicate in splitting it or you will have nothing but crumbs. Eat it hot or cold, but preferably hot, with a spot of strawberry jam and a bit of good old home-cured ham.

These biscuits will keep so well that they are nice for a "traveling lunch." The Confederate Army boys used to carry them and eat them with "a huge relish." This recipe was used in the Stonestreet home in La Plata, Maryland, for years.

Makes about 2 dozen.

Mrs. Mary Stonestreet Lintner, Leesburg, Virginia

VIRGINIA FLAT CAKE

2½ c flour	1 c buttermilk
2 t B.P.	½ t soda
1 t salt	1 t warm water

Add to the sifted-together, dry ingredients the mixed buttermilk, soda, and water. Knead well, and put in a greased, round pan. Score the top of the cake, crisscross fashion. Bake in a hot oven 20-30 minutes.

Serve with hominy, cooked in sausage fat and drenched with cream, and with good country sausage you have a real southern breakfast. This recipe has been used for years in the Davis family. Makes 1 cake.

Mrs. J. B. Davis, Columbus, Ohio

Brown Bread

BAKED BROWN BREAD

1 c Orleans molasses	3 c whole-wheat flour
1 c sour milk	1 c raisins (optional)
1 t salt	1 T shortening (optional)
1 t soda in 1 T warm water	

Mix, in order given. Fill greased, round cans ⅔ full, and bake in a moderately slow oven about 1 hour. This may be baked in any kind of pan, but the round loaf is more attractive. ⅔ c molasses and ⅓ c B. sugar may replace the 1 c molasses, in which case decrease the flour by ½ c. This is a very easy bread to make.

Many's the piece five hungry children have had with great chunks of this bread, freshly churned butter, and cottage cheese, at Aunt Ida's house.

BROWN BREAD

Makes 2-3 round loaves.

Miss Ida M. Lintner, Lyndhurst Farm, Mechanicsburg, Ohio

BOSTON BROWN BREAD

½ c white flour	1 t salt
½ c rye flour	½ c Orleans molasses
1 c corn meal	2 c sour milk
1 c whole-wheat flour	¼ c B. sugar
2 t soda	1 c raisins (optional)

Mix the flours and add the soda and salt. Add the raisins. Mix the molasses, milk, and sugar, and combine the mixtures, blending well. Fill covered, greased cans (coffee cans are good) ⅔ full and steam 3 hours. (See p. 25.) Then dry out the loaves in the uncovered cans in the oven 5-10 minutes.

Real Boston brown is always made of a combination of corn, rye, and wheat. Serve this hot or cold, but best hot with a pot of beans, and you have the perfect Saturday supper.

Makes 2-3 round loaves.

Mrs. Betty Goode Sprague, Cleveland, Ohio

CEREAL BREAD

2 T melted shortening	¼ c milk (about)
1½ c whole-wheat flour	2 T molasses
5 t B.P.	1 beaten egg
1 t salt	1 c cooked cereal
½ c raisins (optional)	

Mix the shortening and dry ingredients. Add the rest of the ingredients, using enough (more-or-less) milk, depending on the stiffness of the cereal, to make a stiff batter. Put in greased loaf pan and let stand 20 minutes. Bake in a moderate oven about 45 minutes.

This is a good way of using leftover cereal if you like a moist bread.

Makes 1 large loaf.

"LEFTOVER" BROWN BREAD

1 c stale bread crumbs	1 c rye flour
1 c rolled oats	1 c graham or whole-wheat flour
1 c thick, sour milk	
1 c water	1 c corn meal
1 c Orleans molasses	1 T soda
1½ c thick, sour milk	1 T salt

Mix the first four ingredients and let them stand overnight. Old muffins or pieces of bread of any kind 'may be used for the crumbs, as they soften up in the milk. In the morning beat the mass until there are no lumps. Add the remaining ingredients in order given. Beat well. Put in large, greased loaf pans and bake in a moderate oven 1-1¼ hours.

This makes an excellent method for using stale bread.

Makes 2 large loaves.

Mrs. H. D. Ashbrook, Granville, Ohio

STEAMED BROWN BREAD

1 c graham or whole-wheat flour	½ c Orleans molasses
1 c white flour	1 c raisins
1 c sour milk	1 t soda dissolved in the milk

Mix in order given, and steam (see p. 25) in 2 greased, covered cans 1½ hours. Dry out the loaves in the uncovered cans in a moderate oven 5-10 minutes.

This is very simple to make and produces a gratifying result. Excellent with a "bean."

Makes 2 loaves.

Mrs. A. S. Martin, Berea, Ohio

SOUTHERN HEALTH BREAD

2 c graham or whole-wheat flour	2 t soda
2 c white flour	1 t salt
2 c bran	3 T lard or chicken fat
½ c sugar	1 c hot water
1 c raisins (or nuts)	1 c Orleans molasses
1 t B.P.	2 c sour milk
	1 beaten egg

Mix the first 8 ingredients in order given. Pour the water over the lard and add the rest of the ingredients. Then combine the mixtures and beat well. Bake in well-greased loaf pans in a moderate oven about 1¼ hours.

This is a health bread with a real flavor appeal. It keeps well.

Makes 3 large loaves.

Mrs. J. E. Sumption, Harrisonburg, Virginia

Coffee Cake

CINNAMON CAKE

1¼ c sugar	5 t B.P.
½ c shortening	½ t salt
2 eggs	1 c raisins or nuts
1½ c milk	(optional)
4 c flour	1 t vanilla

Cream the sugar and shortening. Add the eggs, and beat well. Add the sifted-together, dry ingredients to which the raisins or nuts have already been added, alternately with the milk. Add the vanilla. Put in 2 greased loaf pans and sprinkle well with cinnamon, B. sugar and coconut. Bake in a moderate oven about 25 minutes.

This is an excellent breakfast cake used for years in the Bradfield family.

Makes 2 loaves.

Mrs. Bertha Block Bradfield, Galion, Ohio

COFFEE CAKE

3 c flour	5 t B.P.
1½ c sugar	3 T melted butter
2 t cinnamon	1 beaten egg
½ t salt	1 c milk

Add the butter, egg, and milk to one half the sifted-together, dry ingredients. Save the other half for the top of the cake. Put into greased pie pans. On top, sprinkle the flour mixture you have saved. Dot with butter and a few dashes of cinnamon. Bake in a moderate oven 30-35 minutes.

This is a well-flavored, sweet coffee cake that can be dashed up in a hurry, and it has made its appearance at many Sunday breakfast parties.

Makes 2 round cakes.

Mrs. Marion Thompson Gatrell, Columbus, Ohio

REFRIGERATOR COFFEE CAKE

2 c flour
2 t B.P.
¾ t salt
½ c sugar
6 T shortening

1 beaten egg
½ c milk
1½ T melted butter
4 T sugar
1 T flour
½ t cinnamon

Cut the shortening into the sifted-together, dry ingredients. Add the liquids and blend. Put in well-greased pan (the dough is very stiff). Make a paste of the last 4 ingredients and spread over the top. Bake in a hot oven 25-30 minutes.

This may be made the night before, kept in the refrigerator, and baked in the morning — a great boon to a busy housewife.

Makes 1 cake.

HOT, QUICK COFFEE CAKE

Mrs. Mildred Doyle Burton, Cleveland, Ohio

RICE-FLOUR COFFEE CAKE

1½ c rice flour
¼ t salt
⅓ c sugar
2 t B.P.

2 T melted shortening
1 beaten egg
½ c milk

TOPPING

2 T melted shortening
3 T B. sugar

1 T barley flour
¾ t cinnamon

Mix and sift the dry ingredients. Add the rest in order. Blend. Put in a shallow, greased pan and spread with the topping already mixed together. Bake in a moderately hot oven about 20 minutes.

This is a war-time recipe that is interesting to read and make if you are interested in real recipes used in the time of the

World War I. This makes a rather solid cake with the sandy texture of rice flour. Crumbs may be substituted for the barley flour if it is not available. Do not use this recipe if you want a fluffy coffee cake.

Makes 1 loaf.   *Martha B. Martin*, Kirkwood, Missouri

COFFEE CAKE

1½ c flour	½ c sugar
2 t B.P.	¼ c raisins
⅓ t salt	½ c cream
1 t cinnamon	1 beaten egg

Add the raisins to the sifted-together, dry ingredients. Add the cream and egg, and mix well. Spread in a greased pan and sprinkle with B. sugar, cinnamon, and dots of butter or bits of very thick cream. Bake in a moderate oven 45 minutes. If sour cream is used, add ¼ t soda.

This is an excellent breakfast cake, easily made.

Makes 1 cake.

Mrs. Ada Sumption, Gahanna, Ohio

Corn Bread

They say that man cannot live by bread alone but that, if he has plenty of southern corn bread, he can come mighty close to it. In the South, white corn meal—and if possible it should be burr or water ground—is considered the only thing, while in the North it is considered "aenemic," and the bright yellow is much prefererd. Southerners like their pones, which once were often baked in the hot ashes of the fireplace and called "ash bread," or their "hoe cake," that once was really baked on a hoe in the fireplace or in the fields. Northerners like the johnny-cake, or more fluffy variety. There's an eternal sectional argument about sugar too. It's treason to use it in the South, but the North says that without it corn bread is pretty poor eating. Take your choice.

BRAN-CORN-BACON BREAD

2 beaten eggs	1 t salt
1 T bacon fat	1 t soda
1¼ c milk	1 t B.P.
½ c all bran	1 T sugar
2 c corn meal	¼ lb diced bacon
⅓ c flour	

Combine the eggs, bacon fat, and milk. Add the bran and corn meal. Add the sifted-together, dry ingredients. Mix well. Put into large square pan and sprinkle with the bacon. Bake in a hot oven 25 minutes, and then run it under the broiler flame for about 2 minutes to brown the crust and crisp the bacon.

This is a delightful combination of flavors good with a salad luncheon.

Makes 1 large loaf.

Mrs. Betty Walker Pruitt, Columbus, Ohio

CHARLESTON BATTER BREAD

1 T melted butter	1 c milk
1 c cooked rice or grits	½ c corn meal
⅔ t salt	1 t B.P.
2 beaten eggs	

Mix in order given. Put into a greased baking dish, and bake in a hot oven about 30 minutes.

This is a different bread, like pudding with a layer of corn meal in the bottom. It is good served hot for breakfast.

Makes 1 loaf.

Mrs. J. E. Sumption, Harrisonburg, Virginia

CORN PONE

3 c corn meal	1½ t salt
2 c buttermilk	1 t B.P.
1½ t soda	2 T lard

Mix all in order, and blend well. With the hands, shape "pones" like flat, round cookies. Bake on a greased baking sheet in a moderate oven about 25 minutes or until the edges are brown. Good hot or cold, but best hot.

This recipe has an interesting history. Mrs. Marjorie Barclay McClure told the authors about some excellent pone she had eaten at a restaurant in Greensboro, North Carolina. Since she had forgotten the name of the restaurant, she suggested that we send a letter addressed:

CORN PONE

"To the restaurant that is located in the highest office building in Greensboro that stands on the spot where the old Court House used to be that burned in the fire that everybody in Greensboro remembers."

In two days we had a very helpful letter from the manager, and, not long after that, came a pone for tasting and an apology that it couldn't reach us while still hot!

Makes about 1½ dozen pones.

Mr. J. B. McDonald, Jefferson Roof Restaurant,
Greensboro, North Carolina

CRACKLIN' BREAD

2 c corn meal	1 c cracklings or crisp
1 c boiling water	bacon pieces
	1 t salt

Scald the meal with the water, and add the rest of the ingredients. This should be a stiff dough that can be shaped into pones with the hands. Bake on a greased baking sheet about 20 minutes in a hot oven or until golden brown.

Since cracklings are not often available, the bacon may be used with good results. This bread is crisp and delicious for breakfast, with salad, or almost anytime, if you like the pone type of corn bread.

Makes about 1 dozen.

DODGERS

1⅓ c corn meal (coarse ground best)	⅝ c sour milk or butter-milk (½ c + 2 T)
⅔ c flour	½ t soda
1 t salt	1 beaten egg

Mix the first three; add the sour milk to which the soda has been added. Add the egg. Mix well to a stiff batter. Drop large spoonfuls of batter on to a hot skillet containing about ¼ inch of sizzling bacon fat. Bake on one side 5-8 minutes or until brown; turn and brown on the other side, about 5 minutes. Makes about 8.

Mrs. Ada Morgan Lintner, Linthaven Farm, Powell, Ohio

JOHNNY-CAKE

1½ c corn meal	½ c sugar
2 c flour	2 c milk
2 t B.P.	2 beaten eggs
½ t salt	⅔ c melted shortening

Add the milk, egg, and shortening to the mixed, dry ingredients. Mix well. Bake in a greased, square pan about 30 minutes. Cut in squares and serve at once. Sour milk may be used for the sweet if 1 t soda is added. Very rich sour cream may be used instead of the milk and shortening, and the soda added.

This is the traditional, sweet, rich johnny-cake, well liked in the North. Leftover pieces are delicious split and toasted.

It is interesting to find that in the early days in New England the housewives had a great deal of trouble with the leaven in raised bread. Finally they just gave up trying to make it in winter when the weather was so uncertain and turned to corn bread. Makes 1 large cake.

Mrs. Evelyn Klumb, Cleveland, Ohio

SOUTHERN EGG BREAD

1 c corn meal	½ t B.P.
1 t salt	1 egg
1 T sugar	½ c sour milk
½ t soda	

Mix in order, and put into shallow, greased baking pan. Bake in a hot oven 20-25 minutes.

Makes 1 thin loaf.

Mrs. Pauline Sumption, Harrisonburg, Virginia

SPIDER CORN BREAD

Use the **Southern Egg Bread** recipe (p. 57) and bake it on a spider (shallow skillet) well greased with bacon fat, on top of the stove until it is brown on one side. Turn and brown on the other.

This bread has been made for nearly 40 years in the **Lintner** home. Nothing better with wilted lettuce, a slice of country cured ham, and some homemade cottage cheese.

Makes 1 thin loaf.

Mrs. Ada Morgan Lintner, Linthaven Farm, Powell, Ohio

SPOON BREAD

¾ c corn meal	1 c milk
3 T butter	3 well-beaten eggs
1 t salt	2 t B.P.
1 c boiling water	

Pour the water over the first three ingredients. Cool to luke-warm. Add the remaining ingredients, and beat well. This will be a "queer, watery mess." Pour it into a buttered casserole and bake 40-60 minutes in a moderate oven, until "set."

There's a story that a mammy making mush and corn bread forgot what she was doing, mixed things up badly, and spoon bread was the happy result. It is, as its name implies, not a "finger food." Serve it with maple syrup or just plain. Or, as Mrs. France says, "It is simply swell served with creamed mush-rooms, or creamed chicken or tuna fish, or even dried beef."

Makes 1 medium loaf.

Mrs. Diana Taylor France, Columbus, Ohio

STICKS

1 egg	1 c flour
1 c sour milk	2 t B.P.
½ t soda	1 t salt
1 c corn meal	3 T melted bacon fat

Break the egg in a bowl. Add the milk to which the soda has been added. Add the corn meal and the sifted-together, dry ingredients. Add the bacon fat. Beat all together one minute. Pour into sizzling-hot, corn-stick pans that have been generously greased with bacon fat. Bake in a hot oven about 30 minutes. If sweet milk is used, omit the soda. For a variation, add ½ c, finely cut, soaked, but not cooked, apricots or ½ c whole kernel or fresh corn. This bread may be baked as a loaf or as muffins.

CORN STICKS

Here is a combination of the northern and southern type, and a happy one it is. Mrs. Lewis has given this recipe to many, many people, all of whom pronounce it the best, most foolproof, easiest-to-use recipe they have.

Makes about 14 sticks.

Mrs. Mary Lintner Lewis, Rio Grande, Ohio

SWEET POTATO PONE

1 c finely grated, raw sweet potato	⅓ c boiling water (enough for stiff dough)
1 c corn meal	⅓ t salt

Pour the water over the meal and potato. Add the salt, and mix well. Shape flat pones, and bake on a greased baking sheet in a hot oven about 20 minutes or until they are brown. Chopped raw apple or stewed pumpkin may be substituted for the potato.

These are much like the regular pone, with a different flavor. Makes about 8.

Date Bread

DATE BREAD WITH VARIATIONS

2 c flour	1 c chopped dates
1 t soda	2 c graham flour
3 t B.P.	2 c sour milk
1 t salt	2½ T melted shortening
⅔ c B. sugar	

Sift the first 4 ingredients; add the rest in order. Beat well. Put in greased loaf pans and let stand 20 minutes. Bake in a moderate oven 1 hour.

Cherry-nut bread.—Add ½ c chopped candied cherries and 1 c chopped nuts. Use G. instead of B. sugar.

Date-nut bread.—Add 1 c chopped nuts.

Rye-date-caraway bread.—Use rye flour instead of the graham, and add 2 T caraway seeds. This is a good, crusty bread with a different flavor.

Sour-cream date bread.—Omit the shortening and use 1½ c sour cream for 1½ c of the sour milk.

Makes 2 loaves. *Mrs. Ada Morgan Lintner,* Linthaven Farm, Powell, Ohio

GRAHAM DATE BREAD

2½ c graham or whole-wheat flour	1 t salt
1 c B. sugar	2 T Orleans molasses
1 c chopped dates	2 c sour milk
	1 t soda

Mix the first four ingredients. Mix the remaining, and combine the two. Bake in a greased loaf pan in a moderate oven 45-60 minutes, or steam 1½ hours.

This is quite moist but fine flavored, and cuts well for sandwiches.

Makes 1 large loaf. *Mrs. Mary Nichol Jones,* Granville, Ohio

MOTHER HUBBARD'S DATE BREAD

1 c chopped dates	1 c dark B. sugar
2 T shortening	1 c boiling water
1 t soda	2 c flour
½ t salt	

Pour the boiling water over the dates, shortening, soda, salt, and sugar. Cool. Add the flour, and mix well. Bake in a well-greased pan in a moderate oven 1 hour.

This is very simple to make, easy to slice, costs very little, and is easy to eat. ½ c broken nut meats may be added.

Makes 1 loaf.

Mrs. Mary Alice Kyle, Cleveland, Ohio

STEAMED DATE-BRAN BREAD

2 c flour	1 c large date slices
1 t salt	½ c nuts in large pieces
3 T sugar	1½ c milk
4 t B.P.	1 beaten egg
2 c all bran	2 T melted shortening

Sift the first four ingredients. Add the rest in order given. Put in greased, covered cans or molds, and steam 3 hours. (See p. 25.) Mock steam in half the time, if preferred. Double the amount of dates and nuts, if desired.

This is a moist bread with lots of "character" from the chunks of fruit and nuts that show up in the slices. It is a bit difficult to slice however.

Makes 2 medium loaves.

Mrs. Jean Leet Bargar, Cleveland, Ohio

Doughnuts

According to the Oxford Dictionary, a doughnut is a small, sweet cake fried in hot lard and eaten in the United States and England, especially on Shrove Tuesday. A cruller is the same thing, but twisted and curling, Dutch in origin. We have come to use the two words almost interchangeably.

Many people have heard the story of the doughnut and the hole, and, true or not, it's a good one. A certain little boy, extremely fond of the delicacy, used to stand at his mother's side while she fried doughnuts by the dozen. These were plain, round cakes, well described by the name doughnut. But, hungry ahead of schedule, the little boy always poked the doughy middle out with his thumb, and thus was born the hole in the doughnut!

To qualify as a bread, doughnuts should be served for breakfast, for that is the meal when they are used to replace or supplement the bread plate. Many's the New England home where doughnuts make an almost daily appearance at the breakfast table.

DOUGHNUTS WITH VARIATIONS

1 c sugar	4-5 c flour
1 T butter	1 t nutmeg or cinnamon
2 beaten eggs	3 t B.P.
1 c milk	1 t salt

Cream the sugar and butter. Add the eggs. Add the sifted-together, dry ingredients alternately with the milk. The exact

amount of flour is difficult to determine in doughnuts, but the dough should be soft, yet not too soft to work with. Work with only a portion of dough at a time, keeping the rest in a cool place to prevent tough doughnuts. Roll a sheet about ½-inch thick on a floured board, being careful not to use too much extra flour. Cut in shapes and fry in hot fat. Use a fat kettle that will not tip easily,

DOUGHNUTS

and fill it only half full. If a 1″ cube of stale bread will brown in it in 60 seconds, the fat is ready. Put the doughnuts carefully into the hot fat, being sure not to crowd them. In a few seconds, they will rise to the top, brown on the under side. Turn them, and, as soon as they are well browned all over, remove them to a brown or other porous paper to absorb the excess fat. When they are cool, shake the doughnuts a few at a time in a bag containing a mixture of powdered or granulated sugar and cinnamon, or ice with powdered sugar mixed in hot water to a spreading consistency. Serve at once, as they are best fresh. Incidentally, stale doughnuts, split and toasted, have a charm of their own not appreciated by most people!

Chocolate.—Add 2 T cocoa to the dry ingredients to get the chocolate flavor.

Filled.—Cut plain round doughnuts—no hole; put a teaspoonful of such fillings as stiff jam or jelly, conserve, cooked prunes, figs, or marmalade on one side. Cover with another round. Moisten and pinch the edges together. Put one fork prick on top and fry as above.

Fruit.—Add to the dry ingredients ½ c of such fruits as currants, raisins, etc.

Nuts.—Add to the dry ingredients ½ c chopped nuts.

Sour milk or cream.—Substitute sour milk, and use ½ t soda and only 1 t B.P. Thin, sour cream may be substituted for ½ the milk, and the shortening may then be omitted.

Makes about 3 dozen.

POTATO DOUGHNUTS

4½ c flour	3 eggs
4 t B.P.	1 c sugar
½ t nutmeg	1 c mashed potatoes
½ t soda	2 T melted shortening
1 t salt	¾ c sour milk

Sift together the first five ingredients. Add the sugar to the eggs, and beat well. Add the potatoes and the shortening. Mix all, and then add the dry ingredients alternately with the milk, beating until the batter is smooth. Be careful of overbeating, as the doughnuts will toughen. Chill ½ hour. Follow the directions for doughnuts with variations (p. 62), and you will have a very tender, moist doughnut.

Makes about 3 dozen.

Gingerbread

COLUMBIA UNIVERSITY GINGERBREAD

½ c shortening	2 t soda
½ c sugar	⅓ t salt
1 c Orleans Molasses	1½ t ginger
2 beaten eggs	1 c buttermilk or sour milk
2⅔ c flour	

Cream the shortening and sugar; add the molasses and eggs. Add the sifted-together, dry ingredients alternately with the milk. Bake in a greased loaf pan in a moderate oven about 45-60 minutes. Substitute maple syrup for the molasses for an interesting variation.

This excellent recipe was given to Mrs. Lewis by a cafeteria proprietor at Columbia University.

Makes 1 large loaf.

Mrs. Mary Lintner Lewis, Rio Grande, Ohio

GINGER TEA BREAD

½ c B. sugar	3½ t B.P.
1 c milk	¼ t salt
1 beaten egg	½ c diced crystallized
2¼ c flour	ginger
	½ c melted shortening

Dissolve the sugar in the warmed milk. Cool, and add the egg. To the first mixture add the sifted-together, dry ingredients to which the ginger has been added. Add the shortening and blend. Fill a greased, covered can or mold ⅔ full, and steam 2 hours. (See p. 25.)

This makes a delightfully different, moist tea bread.

Makes 1 large loaf.

Mrs. Mary Lintner Lewis, Rio Grande, Ohio

ICEBOX GINGERBREAD

½ c shortening	3½ c flour
1 c sugar	2 t ginger
1 beaten egg	1 t each, cloves and
1 c Orleans molasses	cinnamon
1 c sour or buttermilk	2 t soda

Cream the sugar and shortening; add the egg, molasses, and milk. Add the sifted-together, dry ingredients. This mixture may be used at once or put in the icebox in a covered bowl and used as desired. Do not keep it over 3 days. Put it in greased loaf pans and bake in a moderate oven 45-60 minutes.

This is a delicious, dark, and flavorful gingerbread. It is good made in individual shapes and served as they do in the South, as a bread with the main meal. There's an old darky cook, Fanny, who used to call these "black mountain muffins."

Makes 2 medium loaves.

Mrs. Virginia Wilkin Marshall, Cleveland, Ohio

Miscellaneous

GUMDROP BREAD

2 well-beaten eggs	½ t cinnamon
¾ c B. sugar	¼ t salt
1 T cold water	½ c chopped nuts or
1 c flour	coconut
1 t B.P.	⅓ c sliced gumdrops, omitting any flavors not liked

Add the sugar and water to the eggs, and beat until thick. Add the nuts and gumdrops to the sifted-together, dry ingredients. Combine mixtures. Bake in a greased shallow pan in a moderately slow oven 40 minutes. Cut in squares or bars, and serve hot or cold.

The assorted gumdrops give a very intriguing appearance to this bread—like fruit cake, but lighter in color. This is good for tea or luncheon, and slices well for thin sandwiches.

Makes 1 small loaf.

Mrs. Mary Alice Kyle, Cleveland, Ohio

FRUIT-BRAN BREAD

1 beaten egg	1 t salt
1 c B. sugar	¾ c coarsely cut dates, rai-
1 c bran	sins, apricots, or any fruit
2 c flour	mixture preferred
1 t soda	¾ c nuts in large pieces
	1 c sour milk

Add the sugar to the egg. Add the bran. Add the sifted-together, dry ingredients to which the fruit and nuts have been added, alternately with the milk. Put in a greased loaf pan and let stand 15 minutes. Bake in a moderate oven 1 hour.

This is a delicious, fruity loaf, excellent most any time and especially good as sandwiches with lots of butter or cream cheese. It lends itself to much variation in flavor.

Makes 1 large loaf.

Mrs. Bertha Bradfield, Galion, Ohio

Muffins

MUFFINS WITH VARIATIONS

Hot muffins for breakfast! Now there's a treat to get a person out of bed even on Sunday morning. You can stir them up with a dash, and, after mastering the simple art of making plain muffins, you can let your imagination work out most tempting variations; for, like biscuits, muffins lend themselves to all sorts of substitutions and additions. Never throw a muffin out. Split and toasted, they are excellent.

BASIC RECIPE

2 c flour	¾ to 1 c milk (depending
4 t B.P.	on amount flour will ab-
½ to 1 t salt	sorb)
2 T sugar (optional)	1 beaten egg
	2 to 3 T melted shortening

Add the mixed liquids to the sifted-together, dry ingredients, stirring the mass only enough to incorporate the liquid with the dry. Muffins must be handled very little, as too much beating and mixing causes a tough product with tunnels in it. Fill greased muffin tins two thirds full of batter and bake in a hot oven 20-25 minutes. Slightly greased paper muffin cups may be put in the muffin tins and the batter put in them if a fancy appearance is liked.

VARIATIONS

MUFFIN VARIATIONS

Applesauce. — Add ⅓ c thick sweetened applesauce and ½ c finely chopped nuts.

Banana bran.—Omit ½ c flour and add 1 c bran or all bran and ½ c mashed banana. These are moist and flavorful.

Candied peel. — Add ½ c finely chopped orange, lemon, citron, or preserved ginger.

Carrot.—Add ½ c grated raw carrot and ½ t grated lemon rind.

Catsup or chili sauce.—Substitute ⅓ c for ⅓ c of the milk called for.

Cheese.—Add last 1 c grated, well-flavored cheese, and sprinkle the tops of the muffins with cheese just before removing them from the oven.

Chocolate.—Add 2 squares of melted chocolate last and increase the sugar to ½ c.

Cocoa.—Add ¼ c cocoa and increase the sugar to ½ c.

Corn.—Add ⅔ c well-drained whole-kernel or grated fresh corn.

Cooked cereal.—Add ½ c. These muffins are always more sticky. The flavor is improved by the addition of ½ c raisins or currants. This is a good way to use leftovers. Rice and grits may be used in the same way.

Creole.—To corn-meal muffins add 1 T finely minced green pepper, 1 t finely minced onion, and ½ c sharply flavored cheese.

Dried fruit.—Add ½ to 1 c finely chopped dates, currants, cooked prunes, figs, or apricots (soaked until plump, but not cooked) to the basic recipe or any of the flour variations (see below).

Fresh fruit.—Be sure that these fruits are drained as dry as possible. Add ½ to 1 c, depending on how fruity a muffin you like, of such fruits as canned or fresh grapefruit, peaches, crushed pineapple, small strawberries, blueberries, cherries, or finely chopped raw apple. These muffins will be more moist than the basic recipe; but they are fine for luncheon, especially if you do not want to serve jam.

Flour variations.—Substitute for 1 c of the flour 1 c of such flours as rye, bran, all bran, corn meal, rice, steel-cut oats, rolled oats, soy-bean meal or flour, buckwheat, whole-wheat, or cracked wheat. Use the 1 c milk, as these flours absorb more liquid. Substitute 2 T of molasses for 2 T of the milk if liked.

Honey.—In the basic recipe or any of the flour variations, substitute ½ c honey for ½ c of the milk. These will have a special flavor.

Jam.—Add ½ to ⅔ c, depending on how much flavor you like, of very stiff jam or marmalade. Pear conserve and orange marmalade are especially good. Omit the sugar.

Maple sugar.—Omit the sugar, and add 1 c crushed maple sugar.

Meat.—Add ½ c, finely chopped dried beef, baked ham, wiener, or crisp bacon. Omit the sugar. Good with salads.

Nut.—Delightfully flavored muffins result from the addition of ½ to 1 c any kind of chopped nuts.

Olive.—Substitute the olive liquid for the milk, and add ½ c finely chopped olives—ripe, green, or stuffed. Omit the sugar and salt. This may sound very odd, but it tastes very good!

Orange.—Substitute ½ c orange juice for ½ c milk; add 1 T grated orange rind and ½ c of any dried fruit or any kind of nuts. Nice for tea.

Peanut butter.—Substitute ¼ c peanut butter for the shortening. Add ½ c finely chopped peanuts if you like the flavor intensified.

Pepper relish.—Add ½ to ⅔ c, and omit the sugar. Any well-drained relish may be used. Odd but good.

Pickle.—Omit the sugar and add ½ c finely chopped sweet or dill pickles. Nothing better for one who likes pickles.

Pumpkin.—Add ½ c cooked, mashed pumpkin.

"Scotch."—Omit the egg, and use water in place of milk.

Sour milk.—Substitute sour or buttermilk for the sweet milk. Use only ½ t B.P. and ½ t soda. This kind of muffin is fine with flours used as suggested under Flour Variations.

Spice.—Add 1 to 2 t, depending on how much flavor you like, of your favorite spice.

Surprise.—Any muffin may be baked sandwich fashion by putting in a shallow layer of batter, then a bit of filling such as a spot of stiff jam, a bit of finely chopped dried fruit, or a sprinkle of nuts. Then put the top shallow layer on and bake as usual. An especially nice surprise is a pitted prune stuffed with a nut and baked in the middle of the sandwich.

Sweet potato.—Add ½ c mashed, cooked sweet potato and ½ c Grape-Nuts if you like. Squash muffins may be made in the same way.

Makes 8-10 medium-sized muffins.

Mrs. Verona Morgan Koby, Graterford, Pennsylvania

Nut Bread

"FIERCE BREAD"

¾ c B. sugar	1 c chopped black walnuts
1 t salt	2 t B.P.
2 c cooking bran	1 t soda
2 c whole-wheat flour	1 beaten egg
	2 c sour milk

Mix in order. Bake in a greased loaf pan in a moderate oven 45-60 minutes.

This is a coarse, delicious kind of whole-wheat nut bread. Be sure to use the black walnuts for the best flavor. Leftover slices are fine, toasted to a sweet "fierceness," according to Miss Alice Robinson of the Fine Arts Department, Ohio State University.

For a less "fierce" product, use 2 c white flour and 2 c whole-wheat. Sweet milk may be used for the sour, if the soda is omitted and the B.P. increased to 4 t. Use 1 c chopped figs for fig nut bread.

Makes 1 large loaf.

Mrs. Betty Walker Pruitt, Columbus, Ohio

NUT BREAD WITH VARIATIONS

2 c sugar	1 t salt
2 T melted shortening	5 c flour
2 c milk	6 t B.P.
2 beaten eggs	2 c chopped nuts

Mix the first 4 ingredients. Add the sifted-together, dry ingredients to which the nuts have been added. Let stand in greased loaf pans 20 minutes, and bake in a moderate oven 1-1½ hours.

This recipe was used for years by Grace Graham Walker of the Home Economics Department, Ohio State University, to make a fine nut bread that can be stirred up in a few minutes, according to her daughter.

Blueberry tea bread.—Add 2 c berries, either canned or fresh. Elderberries may be used.

Butterscotch.—Substitute B. sugar for the G., and use large slices of pecans for the nuts.

Candied fruit.—Add ½ c of chopped, candied fruit peel.

Carrot bread.—Add 1 c drained, cooked, mashed carrots and 1 T grated orange rind.

Catsup or chili-sauce bread.—Substitute catsup or chili sauce for the milk.

Conserve bread.—Add ½ c very stiff conserve or marmalade.

Crumb bread.—Substitute very fine, dry bread crumbs for ½ the flour.

Grape-Nuts bread.—Substitute Grape-Nuts for the nuts.

Olive bread.—Omit the sugar, and add 2 c chopped, ripe, plain or stuffed olives.

Peanut-butter bread.—Add 2 c peanut butter, and use ½ c less flour. Use peanuts for the nuts.

Makes 2 small loaves.

Mrs. Betty Walker Pruitt, Columbus, Ohio

RAISIN-NUT BREAD

2 T shortening	2 t soda
1½ c light B. sugar	2 c boiling water
½ t salt	3 c flour
2 beaten eggs	1 t B.P.
2 c raisins	1 c chopped black walnuts

Cream the shortening and sugar. Add the salt and eggs. Pour the soda and water over the raisins and let stand till cool. Add to the first mixture. Add the sifted-together, dry ingredients to which the nuts have been added. Bake in greased loaf pans, in a moderate oven, 1 hour.

This is a delicious, moist bread that keeps well and makes wonderful sandwiches, especially with creamed cheese.

Makes 1 large loaf.

Mrs. A. P. Sumption, Harrisonburg, Virginia

Orange Bread

HONEY-ORANGE BREAD

1 c finely ground orange
   peel (about 3 orange
   rinds)
2 c water
½ t salt
1 c honey and ¼ c water

2 beaten egg yolks
1 c milk
3 c flour
3 t B.P.
½ c chopped nuts (or
   rolled oats)

Boil the first three ingredients until the rind is soft. Drain and boil in the honey and water mixture until very thick. Mix the egg yolks and milk. Add the sifted-together, dry ingredients to which the nuts have been added. Add the honey-orange mixture cooled to lukewarm. Put in a greased loaf pan, and bake in a moderate oven 1 hour.

This bread is better the day after baking. It will keep fresh for a week if you wrap it in waxed paper. The honey keeps it moist. Children find this a favorite, and grown-ups like it for tea. Makes 2 medium loaves.

Mrs. Mary Lintner Lewis, Rio Grande, Ohio

ORANGE OR LEMON BREAD

1 c finely chopped orange
   or lemon peel
1 c water
1 c sugar
1 t salt
1 c milk

¼ c orange or lemon juice
1 t vanilla
3½ c flour
3½ t B.P.
½ t nutmeg (optional)

Cook the first 4 ingredients together 8-10 minutes. Cool. Add the rest in order, the dry ingredients sifted together. Put in a greased loaf pan and let rise 10 minutes. Bake in a moderate oven 1 hour.

This is a moist, rather solid bread, since it contains no shortening. Because it will slice thin, it is good for dainty sandwiches. Makes 2 loaves.

Mrs. H. D. Ashbrook, Granville, Ohio

ORANGE MARMALADE BREAD

3 c flour	1 T grated orange rind
3 t B.P.	½ c orange marmalade
½ t salt	1 c milk
¼ c sugar	1 beaten egg
½ c chopped nuts	

To the sifted-together, dry ingredients add the nuts and orange rind. Combine the marmalade, milk, and egg, and add to the first mixture. Mix well. Put in a greased loaf pan and bake 1 hour in a moderate oven.

This has a special flavor due to the marmalade-nut combination. Makes 2 small loaves.

Mrs. A. S. Martin, Berea, Ohio

RICH ORANGE-MARMALADE LOAF

3 c flour	1 T grated orange rind
2 t B.P.	⅓ c orange marmalade
⅔ t soda	3 T orange juice
1 t salt	1 beaten egg
½ c sugar	1 c sour cream (if very
⅓ c pecans	rich, omit shortening)
	2 T melted shortening

Sift the dry ingredients, and add the rest in order. Mix well. Put in greased loaf pans and bake in a moderately slow oven about 50 minutes.

"They serve this bread out here with hot spiced drinks or hot tea."

Makes 2 small loaves.

Mrs. Russel Squire, Los Angeles, California

Pancakes

PANCAKES WITH VARIATIONS

These go by various names according to the section of the country. Griddlecakes, flapjacks, battercakes, hot cakes, and slapjacks are all the same, made from a thin, "pour batter" and cooked—fried, or "baked," as some say—on a hot griddle, spider, or frying pan. An electric sandwich grill serves nicely if one likes to make the cakes at the table. Be sure the pan is very hot, and pour in just enough batter to make cakes about 3 inches in diameter. Usually four can be made at once in a normal-sized pan. The pan must be greased after each batch, or the cakes stick, but be sure to grease lightly, using any fat but butter, as butter causes things to stick. The good, old-time method was to run a bacon rind over the griddle, and this is still a good method, but with sliced bacon the fashion, most people are not blessed with bacon rinds. When the pancake begins to bubble on the topside, carefully lift the edge with the turner and you'll see that the undersurface is brown. Then carefully—and this is an art not to be taken lightly—flip the cake onto its other side. In a few minutes, and this is something you must learn by experience only, the cake will be done. Never "spank" the cake with the turner just to be sure you are doing the right thing by it, for that will surely make it tough. Serve it at once. Whatever may be said for the romance of "a stack of wheats," the practical side demands that cakes not be stacked, for they sweat and become clammy.

Serve pancakes whenever, with whatever, your heart desires. If you are a southerner, you'll swear by ribbon cane; if a northerner, maple syrup is the only thing, but jelly, brown-sugar syrup, and corn syrup all have their advocates.

BASIC RECIPE

2½ c flour	1 beaten egg
1 t soda	2 T melted shortening
½ t salt	1 T sugar
2 c sour or buttermilk (or sour cream)	

Add the milk to the sifted-together, dry ingredients. Then add the egg, melted shortening, and sugar. Mix well, but not too much.

Leftover batter may be covered, put in the icebox, and saved a few days. If it is too stiff, add a little more milk.

Nothing better for breakfast.

There are many variations, some of which may be combined. You may have to use more milk, as flours absorb different amounts of liquid, but the cake will not be harmed by the addition.

VARIATIONS

Applesauce.—Substitute 1 c unsweetened applesauce for 1 c milk. This will be more moist than the basic recipe. Add 2 t cinnamon for extra flavor.

Banana.—Add ½ c mashed banana and 2 T sugar.

Bread-crumb.—Substitute 1 c dry bread crumbs for 1 c of flour.

Buckwheat.—Substitute 1 c buckwheat flour for 1 c of white. For "old-fashioned buckwheats," which are far superior, see under **Yeast Bread in Small Forms (p. 110).**

Cereal.—Substitute 1 c cooked cereal or grits for 1 c flour. These are moist.

Corn.—To some people these are superior to any other cake. Substitute 1½ c corn meal for 1½ c flour called for.

Honey.—Use honey or molasses in place of sugar. Brown sugar may be used for granulated.

Huckleberry or blueberry.—Add 2 c berries. Nothing better than these for a breakfast cooked in the open, especially in Vermont.

Rye.—Substitute rye flour for half the white flour.

Whole-wheat.—Substitute half whole-wheat flour for the white flour.

Sweet milk.—Use in place of sour milk. Omit the soda and add 5 t B.P.

Makes about 36 cakes.

Leland Samsel, Ashland, Ohio

Popovers

POPOVERS WITH VARIATIONS

1 c flour	2 beaten eggs
⅓ t salt	1 t melted shortening
1 c milk	

Mix flour and salt. Add the milk gradually. Add the eggs and shortening. Beat the batter 5 minutes with an egg beater or 3 with an electric mixer. Fill sizzling hot, greased, iron popover pans, or cold, greased, glass ramekins half full of batter. Bake in a hot oven 30 minutes. Reduce the heat to moderate, and continue baking 15 minutes to dry out the inside somewhat. Do not open the door for the first 15 minutes of baking, or the popovers may not "pop."

POPOVERS

Popovers are like a cream puff, less "eggy" and less sweet. They are traditional Sunday-morning bread in some homes. They should always be served piping hot with lots of butter and good jam.

Cheese.—Add ½ c grated American cheese and 2 more eggs.

Rye, whole-wheat, or graham popovers.—Use ⅔ c of these flours for ⅔ c of the white flour called for.

Makes 8-10.

Sally Broughton, Cleveland, Ohio

Prune Bread

BRAN PRUNE BREAD

1 c bran	1 c flour
1 c sour cream	½ t soda
½ c chopped, cooked prunes	1 t B.P.
1 T molasses	½ t salt
½ c sugar	

Mix the first five ingredients. Add the sifted-together, dry ingredients. Put in a greased loaf pan and bake in a moderate oven 1 hour. This may be baked in a covered glass dish with the lid slightly ajar for a mock steaming. Then serve it hot for dinner, leave it in the covered dish, and reheat it for a very fine breakfast bread.

Makes 1 loaf.

Mrs. Fernand Pierre Brasseur, Cleveland, Ohio

ORANGE PRUNE BREAD

3 c flour	1 c ground, pitted, un-
4 t B.P.	cooked prunes
½ t soda	2 T finely cut orange peel
1½ t salt	½ c chopped nuts
2 T sugar	1 c milk
	2 beaten eggs
	¼ c melted shortening

To the sifted-together, dry ingredients, add the prunes, orange peel, and nuts. Mix the milk, eggs, and shortening, and add. Blend well. Bake in a greased loaf pan in a moderate oven about 1 hour.

The nuts and orange give this bread a special flavor. A good tea bread.

Makes 1 large loaf.

Mrs. Betty Goode Sprague, Cleveland, Ohio

PRUNE JUICE BREAD

1 c sugar	1 c chopped, cooked prunes
1 beaten egg	1½ c flour
½ c thick prune juice	1½ t B.P.
1 c sour cream	½ t salt
1 c whole-wheat flour	1 t soda
1 c chopped nuts	

Combine the first 4 ingredients. Add the whole-wheat flour, nuts, and prunes. Add the sifted-together, dry ingredients. Bake in a greased loaf pan in a moderate oven about 1 hour.

This is like a health bread, but with so excellent a flavor and texture that it is popular on any tea table and for any child's piece.

Makes 2 loaves.

Laurabelle Ashbrook, Cleveland, Ohio

Salad or Soup Accompaniments

CORN-CHEESE STRIPS

1½ c corn meal	2 beaten eggs
1½ c sour milk	¾ t soda
2 T bacon dripping (or other shortening)	1 T water
	1 c grated, snappy cheese
1 t salt	

Cook the first four ingredients in a double boiler about 20 minutes. Cool. Stir in the eggs and soda dissolved in the water. Mix. Add the cheese. Spread thin on a greased baking sheet, and bake in a moderate oven about 40 minutes, or until the edges are brown. Mark in strips and serve. These may be toasted when left over and are even better than the first time.

Makes about 2 dozen.

Mrs. Fernand Pierre Brasseur, Cleveland, Ohio

CHEESE PUFFS

½ c boiling water	½ c flour
⅓ t salt	1 egg
1 T butter	3 T grated cheese

To the boiling water add the salt and butter. Add the flour, and beat well. Add the egg, and beat again. Add the cheese, and drop by teaspoonful on a greased baking sheet. Bake in a hot oven 15 minutes.

These should be very small, but if you prefer larger ones, bake them 15-20 minutes longer in a slow oven. They are delicious filled with cheese and nuts, minced chicken, or finely chopped celery and salad dressing.

Makes 8 small puffs.

CHEESE STRAWS

½ c flour	2 T water
2 T butter	1 beaten egg
¼ t salt	½ c very snappy, grated cheese (Parmesan is good)
¼ t pepper	

Cut the butter into the flour. Add the rest in order. Roll thin, cut in strips, and bake in a hot oven 5-8 minutes or until brown.

Leftover pie crust with the addition of the cheese will serve as a good substitute.

You may brush the tops with slightly beaten egg white and sprinkle with grated cheese or seeds, such as celery or caraway or both.

Makes about 1 dozen.

CHEESE SALAD WAFERS

1 c flour	cold water for stiff dough
½ t salt	¼ c grated cheese
½ t B.P.	paprika

Make a dough of the first four ingredients. Roll thin. Sprinkle with the cheese and paprika. Fold each end to the center and the sides to the center, and roll again to ⅛-inch thickness. Roll as a jelly roll, and slice thin. Bake in a hot oven on a greased baking sheet about 8 minutes.

These are delicious and crisp in spite of the fact that there is no shortening.

Makes about 1 dozen.

Mrs. Carlotta Patterson Thayer, Avon Park, Florida

CORN-LACE PUFFS

½ c boiling water	½ c corn meal
½ t salt	2 egg whites

Mix the first three, cool, and fold in the stiffly beaten egg whites. Drop by teaspoonfuls on greased baking sheet, and bake in a moderate oven about 30 minutes.

Add 3 T cooked, crumbled sausage for a variation.

Makes about 8.

Mrs. Fernand Pierre Brasseur, Cleveland, Ohio

HOMEMADE CRACKERS

2 c flour	1 t salt
2 t butter	1 beaten egg
2 t lard	½ c milk

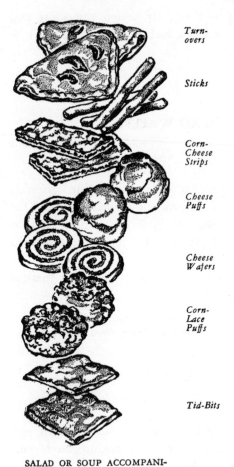

Turn-overs

Sticks

Corn-Cheese Strips

Cheese Puffs

Cheese Wafers

Corn-Lace Puffs

Tid-Bits

SALAD OR SOUP ACCOMPANI-
MENTS

Rub the shortening into the flour. Add the rest in order. Mix. Roll very thin. Cut round. Prick with a fork, sprinkle with salt, and bake on a greased baking sheet in a hot oven about 5 minutes.

Makes about 3 dozen.

PULLED BREAD

For a quickly made and delicious bread, cut the crusts off a loaf of bread, and "pull" thick slices off with two forks. Brown in a hot oven, and serve at once with plenty of butter.

Makes about 12 slices.

Mrs. Hazel Wisch Ashbrook,
Newark, Ohio

QUICK-DELIVERY HOT BREAD

Carefully cut the crusts from three sides and both ends of a loaf of bread. Slice the loaf, being careful not to cut through the bottom crust. Butter each slice and put in a moderately hot oven until delicately brown on the outside. This is an attractive and delicious loaf. It saves time for the weary hostess who cannot bother with a more complicated bread.

Makes about 12 slices.

Mrs. Fernand Pierre Brasseur, Cleveland, Ohio

SALAD TURNOVERS

1½ packages cream cheese	¼ c butter
1 c flour	1 t B.P.

Mix well. Let stand in refrigerator all night. Roll thin. Cut in 3-inch squares. Fill with marmalade, or lobster, tuna, salmon, or chicken, moistened with salad dressing. Bring the edges together to make a triangle. Moisten and pinch the edges. Bake on a greased baking sheet in a hot oven about 10 minutes. Serve hot or cold. Delicious!

Makes about 6.   *Mrs. Mary Alice Kyle,* Cleveland, Ohio

SAVORY BREAD

Follow the directions for Quick-Delivery Hot Bread, using a French bread and not removing the crust. Spread with butter that has been allowed to stand overnight with a clove of garlic, or a piece of onion, or mixed with celery seeds or herbs. This is a very special delicacy for those who like high flavors.

SOUTHERN PUFFS

Roll any biscuit dough thin, and cut into 1-inch-wide, finger lengths. Fry in deep fat until a golden brown. Nothing better served hot with chicken.

Makes about 1 dozen.

Mrs. Mary Lou Bradfield Brasseur, Cleveland, Ohio

TIDBITS

1 egg white	⅛ t Worcestershire Sauce
¼ t salt	½ c grated cheese
⅛ t pepper	

Add the salt to the egg white and beat until very stiff. Add the rest in order, and spread on thin squares of bread or homemade crackers (p. 80). Brown in a hot oven, and serve at once.

Mrs. Susan Hays Ashbrook, Granville, Ohio

Sally Lunn

PLAIN SALLY LUNN

2 T melted shortening	2 t B.P.
1 c milk	½ t salt
3 eggs, beaten separately	2 T sugar
2 c flour	

Add the melted shortening and milk to the beaten egg yolks. Add the sifted-together, dry ingredients. Mix. Fold in the stiffly beaten egg whites. Bake in a greased shallow pan in a moderate oven 30-40 minutes.

Serve this at once as a delicious hot bread for dinner or luncheon. Break it in squares. Cutting with a knife will make it soggy.

Makes 1 loaf.

Mrs. Betty Goode Sprague, Cleveland, Ohio

WHOLE-WHEAT SALLY LUNN

½ c shortening	1 T B.P.
½ c sugar	¾ t salt
3 beaten eggs	1 c whole-wheat flour
1 c flour	1 c milk

Cream the shortening and sugar. Add the eggs and beat well. Add the sifted-together, dry ingredients and the whole-wheat flour alternately with the milk. Bake in a greased shallow pan in a hot oven 20 minutes.

Serve hot with plenty of butter. Fine for those who do not care for white-flour breads.

Makes 1 loaf.

Sally Broughton, Cleveland, Ohio

Waffles

"The word waffle can be traced to a Dutch word spelled 'wafel.' It is dated as far back as 1817 in Murray's Oxford Dictionary, where it is described as a 'soft cake of German extraction.'

"In the United States the popularity of waffles has long been established, for we find them in various forms as a welcome part of any meal. Noth-

ing is more interesting than Sunday morning breakfast with company enjoying waffles, plain or 'different' with various toppings. They are a means of entertaining guests no matter what hour of the day. Waffle parties are so easy for the hostess without a maid, for when the batter

WAFFLE

is mixed, extras ready, and the table set, her work is over, and the host takes up his part of the entertainment—full charge of the baking and serving.

"All waffle recipes may be made up ahead of time and placed in a covered container in a mechanical refrigerator ready for use unless otherwise stated in the recipe. Never throw away any leftover batter, as it will keep for about a week in a refrigerator. It is not necessary to add B.P. to leftover batter, but if it has stiffened add a little milk to return it to its original consistency, and bake as usual. Add just enough milk to allow the batter to drop swiftly from the spoon. More is unnecessary and will detract from the crispness.

"Most new waffle irons have manufacturers' instructions attached. However, if these are lacking, before using the first batter, heat the iron, well greased with any unsalted fat, slowly till it is smoking. Pour batter, being careful not to run it over, and bake until the waffle is well browned. Throw this waffle away. Usually the iron will stick no more, but if it should, this process may be repeated. After this, never grease the iron again. Never wash it; just wipe off the outside.

"Always have it smoking hot before the first waffle goes in. If the iron is automatic, follow the baking instructions; if not, time the first one, and estimate thereafter from that. Do not lift the top of the iron unless it lifts easily.

"No matter how old the iron, the first waffle never seems to be quite as crisp as later ones; so be sure it never goes to the guest of honor.

"There has been no mention of how many waffles these recipes will make, for there are so many varying sizes of waffle irons that it is impossible to exactly estimate. Most of them will serve about 6 people."

Dorothy Lintner Pritchard, Columbus, Ohio

The authors are indeed indebted to their sister and brother-in-law, Mr. and Mrs. S. C. Pritchard, for this entire section on waffles. They have spent an endless amount of time testing and tasting and retesting and retasting, so that we look upon them as authorities in this waffle business. All of the recipes are their own developments unless other credit is given.

PLAIN WAFFLES

2 c flour	2 eggs, beaten separately
3 t B.P.	1¼ c milk
½ t salt	6 T melted shortening

Add the well-beaten egg yolks, milk, and melted shortening to the sifted-together, dry ingredients. Mix well. Carefully fold in the stiffly beaten egg whites, and bake without any further mixing of the batter.

The procedure in an electric mixer is as follows: Beat the eggs, yolks, and whites together 1 minute at high speed. Add the milk, and beat one minute longer. Add the sifted-together, dry ingredients, and beat one more minute at high speed. Add the melted shortening, and beat 15 seconds or until the mixture is well blended.

WAFFLE TOPPINGS

Sugar syrup, maple syrup, sorghum, honey, melted butter mixed with crushed pineapple, cream cheese, powdered sugar, jelly, crushed fresh or dried fruit, ice cream, creamed meats, vegetables, sea foods, or eggs may be used as toppings.

Plain waffles may be "dressed up" with the addition to the batter of diced, crisp bacon, fresh or canned corn, grated cheese, or nuts before baking. Here are a number of different waffles that have been tested for just the right amount of extras to add.

CHEESE WAFFLES

Add 1 c grated cheese, and omit 2 T shortening in the recipe for plain waffles.

CLABBER WAFFLES

2 c flour	2 c clabber, sour milk, or
2 t soda	buttermilk
¼ t salt	1 egg (beaten separately)
	4 T melted shortening
	(bacon dripping good)

Plain-waffle method. These are the least expensive and the most filling waffles. This recipe surely proves that butter is not necessary to make crisp waffles, for these are crisp. These are good with ½ c fresh or canned corn added to the batter before baking.

For corn-meal waffles, substitute ¾ c corn meal for ¾ c of flour called for. 2 T sugar may be added.

Mrs. Dorothy Criswell Price, Evergreen Farm, Newark, Ohio

CORN-MEAL WAFFLES, VIRGINIA STYLE

1½ c boiling water
½ c white corn meal
3 c flour
3 T sugar
3 t B.P.

½ t salt
1½ c milk
2 eggs (beaten separately)
3 T melted shortening

Cook the corn meal slowly in the boiling water 30 minutes. Add to the dry ingredients, and proceed as for plain waffles. Bake a little longer than plain waffles. These are very good for people who like the corn-meal flavor without the grittiness.

CORN-MEAL WAFFLE MIX

4 c flour
3 c corn meal
4 T B.P.

2 t salt
4 T sugar

Sift all together and store in a tight jar until ready for use. To serve two or three people use:

1 c waffle mix
1 egg (beaten separately)

¾ c milk
2 T melted shortening

Mix as for plain waffles. These are very good for a hearty breakfast on a cold morning. People who like the gritty, corn-meal flavor will call for more.

MASHED-POTATO WAFFLES

Follow the recipe for sweet-potato waffles (p. 87), omitting the cinnamon.

MOLASSES BUCKWHEAT WAFFLES

1 c flour
1 c buckwheat flour
1 t B.P.
¾ t salt
½ t soda

2 eggs (beaten separately)
1 c sour milk
¼ c milk (more if necessary)
6 T melted shortening
3 T Orleans molasses

Mix as plain waffles, adding molasses with egg yolks. These are very substantial; men like them.

NON-BUTTER, SOUR-CREAM WAFFLES

1 c flour	¾ c rich, sour cream
¾ t soda	¾ c buttermilk
1 t B.P.	2 eggs (beaten separately)
1 t salt	

Follow plain-waffle procedure.

RICE OR CEREAL WAFFLES

2 c flour	2 T sugar (optional)
1 t salt	2 eggs (beaten separately)
3 t B.P.	4 T melted shortening
1 c cooked rice, grits, or leftover cereal	1½ c milk (more if necessary)

Plain-waffle procedure, adding rice to liquid ingredients. Mix just before serving, as the batter does not keep well. Bake longer than plain waffles. These make a good luncheon or supper dish, with butter.

¾ c rice flour may be substituted for ¾ c of the flour.

SWEET-POTATO WAFFLES

1¼ c cake flour	2 eggs (beaten separately)
4 t B.P.	1 c mashed sweet potato
⅛ t cinnamon	1 c milk
2 T sugar	½ c melted butter
¼ t salt	

Plain-waffle procedure, adding the sweet potato with the beaten egg yolk.

Make just before serving, as they do not keep well.

These are delicious and make a complete meal when served with fried ham and pineapple, and green beans.

Yeast Bread in Loaves

BRAN BREAD

1 cake yeast	5 c flour
2 t salt	3 c bran
⅓ c dark corn syrup	2 T melted shortening
2 c scalded and cooled milk	

Crumble the yeast in a bowl. Add salt, syrup, and milk. Add 3 c of the flour. Beat well. Add the shortening and bran, then the rest of the flour, and knead well. Put in a greased bowl, turning the dough several times so all sides are coated with grease. Let rise till double in bulk. Punch down and let rise again. Shape in loaves. Put in greased loaf pans and let rise till double in bulk. Bake 15 minutes in a hot oven and 45 in a moderate.

When this bread was baked in a large, flat, sheet-iron pan, it was called "slab" bread and was popular in the Lintner family for after-school pieces if sliced in pieces an inch thick and at least a foot long and buttered as thickly as the bread.

Variations may be secured by substituting for the bran: barley flour, buckwheat, corn meal, cracked wheat, graham, rolled or steel-cut oats, whole wheat, or soy-bean flour. One or two cups of any combination of dried fruit or nuts may be added for special flavors. Makes 2 large loaves or 1 "slab."

Mrs. Ada Morgan Lintner, Linthaven Farm, Powell, Ohio

CEREAL BREAD

1 c warm cooked cereal, grits, or fine hominy	1 T shortening
1½ t salt	½ cake yeast
2 T sugar	4 T lukewarm water
	2½-3 c flour

Add salt, sugar, and shortening to cereal. Mix yeast and water and add. Add 1 c of the flour. Mix well. Let rise until double in bulk. Add the rest of the flour and knead. Let rise again till double in bulk. Knead again. Put in greased loaf pans and let rise till double again. Bake in a hot oven 10 minutes, and in a moderate 50 more.

Makes 2 medium loaves.

CHEESE BREAD

2 T sugar	1 t sugar
1½ t salt	2 T lukewarm water
1 c milk	1 beaten egg
1 cake yeast	1 c grated cheese
	3-4 c flour

Add the sugar and salt to the milk. Add the t of sugar and water to the yeast. Let stand 5 minutes, and add to the first mixture. Add the egg and the cheese. Add the flour, using only enough to knead easily. Knead about 5 minutes on a floured board, until the dough is elastic. Put in a greased loaf pan and let rise until double in bulk. Bake 10 minutes in a hot oven and 50 in a moderate.

For pimiento-cheese bread add ½ c finely chopped pimientos, or substitute pimiento cheese for that called for.

This is an excellent, different bread, particularly good for sandwiches and toast.

Makes 1 large loaf.

Mrs. Sylvia Kuechle, Cleveland, Ohio

MARY'S BREAD WITH VARIATIONS

2 cakes yeast	5 t salt
2½ T sugar	2 T melted shortening
3½ c liquid (½ evaporated milk, ½ water)	10 c flour

Crumble the yeast in a bowl. Add the sugar, and let stand until yeast is liquified. Add the milk—scalded and cooled—salt, and shortening. Add all the flour, and work in with the hands. Knead well and let rise until double in bulk (about 2 hours). Knead and let rise again until double (about 1 hour). Put in greased loaf pans, and let rise until double in bulk (about 1½ hours). Bake in a hot oven 10 minutes and then a moderate 50 more.

For a very interesting crust known as "salty top," rub the hot, baked bread with butter, and shake over it a thick layer of salt. This will all be absorbed, but keep on with the salt until no more can be absorbed. This crust will be about ⅛-inch thick.

Fruit bread.—2 c of any chopped, dried fruits such as raisins, currants, dates, or nuts or any combination of these may be added for variation. Increase the sugar to ½ c, and ice with C. sugar mixed with water to a spreading consistency.

Buttermilk bread.—Use half buttermilk and half water for the liquid. Add 1 t soda. This makes a very tender bread. Whey may be used in the same way.

Cocoa bread.—Add 2 c cocoa and 4 beaten eggs. Children especially like this.

Bread sticks.—Long, pencil-like strips brushed with beaten egg, and sprinkled with seeds if desired, make a very good stick to serve with soup. Bake about 10 minutes in a hot oven.

Makes 4 loaves.

Whole wheat, cracked wheat, or graham.—Substitute 3 c of either for white flour.   *Mrs. Mary Lintner Lewis,* Rio Grande, Ohio

NAYLOR BREAD WITH VARIATIONS

½ c sugar	2 c milk, scalded and
2 beaten eggs	cooled
2 cakes yeast	½ c melted shortening
2 t salt	8-10 c flour

Mix sugar and eggs. Add crumbled yeast, and beat with egg beater until smooth. Add the salt, the milk, the shortening, and the flour, using only enough to make a dough that will handle, as this should be a tender bread. Knead well. Let rise till double in bulk. Punch down. Put in greased bread pans, let rise till double in bulk, and bake in a hot oven 10 minutes and then in a moderate 40 more. This should be light and tender, somewhat like kuchen dough.

Cinnamon bread.—Roll out 1-inch thick. Sprinkle with brown sugar and cinnamon, and dot with butter. Roll as for jelly roll, and place in greased pan with the seam at the bottom. Let rise till double in bulk, and bake as above.

Long Johns.—To the above add 2 T butter, 2 T sugar, 1 c currants. Shape long, sticklike rolls. Dip them in melted butter. Place on a baking sheet about 1 inch apart, and let rise till double in bulk. They will flatten out a little as they rise. Excellent with a luncheon or supper.

Chunk bread.—Break off irregular chunks of dough, and fry in deep fat till golden brown. Tradition says that these chunks were made long in the Washington home, called "fried bread," and served as a breakfast delicacy.

Makes 2 loaves.

Mrs. Carrie Naylor, Cleveland, Ohio

ORANGE BREAD

1 cake yeast	2 T sugar
¾ c lukewarm water	2 grated orange rinds
1 beaten egg	¾ c orange juice
2 T melted shortening	4 c flour
1 t salt	

Dissolve the yeast in the water. Add the egg, shortening, salt, sugar, orange rind, and juice. Stir the flour in, and beat until smooth. Add more flour if necessary in kneading. Let rise till double in bulk. Put in greased loaf pan and let rise again till double. Bake in a hot oven 10 minutes and then in a moderate 50 more.

The orange juice and rind make this an excellent bread, good for sandwiches.

Makes 1 loaf.

Mrs. A. S. Martin, Berea, Ohio

PRUNE BREAD

2 c milk, scalded and
   cooled
1 cake yeast
¼ c melted shortening
2 t salt

2 c chopped, cooked prunes
¾ c bran
¼ c sugar
7-8 c flour

Crumble the yeast in the milk. Add the rest in order given. Knead well. Let rise till double in bulk. Punch down. Let rise again and then put in greased loaf pans. Let rise again until double, and bake in a hot oven 10 minutes and then in a moderate 50 more.

For a more "pruney" flavor, use 1 c prune juice in place of 1 c milk.

For an extra flavor add 1 c nut meats.

Makes 2 large loaves.

ROLLED-OAT HONEY BREAD

1 cake yeast
½ c lukewarm water
2 c quick-cook, rolled
   oats
2 c boiling water

2 T shortening
½ c honey (light corn syrup
   may be substituted)
4-5 c flour
2 t salt

Soften yeast in water. Add 1 T of the flour, and let stand 10 minutes. Scald the oats with the boiling water and add the shortening and honey; set aside until lukewarm. Combine the two mixtures and add 1 c of the flour. Beat well. Let rise 1 hour. Add the rest of the flour and the salt. Knead. Let rise till double in bulk.

Put in greased loaf pans and let rise till double in bulk. Bake in a hot oven 10 minutes and then in a moderate 45 more.

Add 1 c chopped dates or 1 c nuts for a variation.

Makes 2 medium loaves.

SALT-RISING BREAD

1 c milk, scalded and
   cooled
1 t salt
1 T sugar

2 T corn meal (white
   preferred)
1 T butter
3 c flour (for 1 loaf)

Add the salt, sugar, corn meal, and butter to the milk. Place this in a glass fruit jar or a heavy crockery pitcher and surround it with water about 120 F. Allow it to stand 6-7 hours or until it starts to ferment. If it has "worked" enough, the gas can be heard as it escapes. This leaven contains enough liquid for 1 loaf. If more loaves are wanted, add 1 c water, 1 t salt, 1 T sugar, and 1 T butter for each additional loaf. Make a soft sponge by adding 1 c flour for each loaf to be made. Beat well. Put the sponge to rise again at 120 F. When it is very light, add more flour (2 c flour each loaf) gradually so that the dough can be kneaded and not stick to hands. Knead 10-15 minutes. Put in a greased pan. Let rise until 2½ times its original size. Bake in hot oven 15 minutes and then in a moderate 45 more.

Notice that there is no yeast in this bread except the wild yeast that comes from the air. While it is baking there is a disagreeable odor that disappears when the bread is baked. It always has a peculiar flavor, disliked by some and prized by others.

It is never so light as the bread made with yeast. A loaf made with 1 c liquid will not rise to the top of a standard-sized bread pan. Do not try to keep this fine-grained, white bread long, as it dries out.

Makes 1 loaf.

SHREDDED-WHEAT BREAD

2 Shredded Wheat Biscuit	1 T sugar
(1 c crushed)	1 T shortening
1 c boiling water	½ cake yeast
¼ c dark corn syrup	2 T water
½ t salt	3 c flour (about)

Mix the crushed Shredded Wheat with the next 5 ingredients. Cool. Soften the yeast with the water and add to the first mixture. Add the flour, and mix well. Let rise till double in bulk. Knead. Put in greased loaf pans, let rise till double in bulk, and bake in a hot oven 10 minutes and then in a moderate 50 more.

Grape-Nuts may be substituted for the Shredded Wheat.

One cup of any chopped, dried fruit or nuts, or a combination, adds flavor.

Makes 2 medium loaves.

Mrs. Helen Shephard Ashbrook, Washington, D. C.

WAR BREAD

1 c milk	½ cake yeast
1 c rolled oats	¼ c lukewarm water
2 T sugar	½ c white flour
1 t salt	½ c whole-wheat flour
1 T shortening	1 c rye, buckwheat, or corn meal

Scald the milk and add to it the next 4 ingredients. Cool. Soften the yeast with the water and add to the first mixture. Add the flours and knead. Let rise till double in bulk. Punch down and let rise again till double. Put in greased loaf pan, let rise till double in bulk, and bake in hot oven 10 minutes and then in a moderate 50 more.

This is the type of "substitute" bread so much used during World War I.

Makes 1 large loaf.

Mrs. A. S. Martin, Berea, Ohio

Yeast Bread in Small Forms

BUN-DOUGH ROLLS WITH VARIATIONS

⅓ c sugar	1 beaten egg
⅓ c butter	1 cake yeast
1 T salt	¼ c lukewarm water
1 c scalded milk	3-4 c flour

Pour the milk over the first three ingredients, and cool to lukewarm. Add the egg and the yeast mixed with the water. Add the flour, using only enough for a soft dough that can be stirred with a spoon. Let rise till double in bulk. Punch down. Make into rolls, using more flour if necessary to handle. Place, just touching, on a greased pan with sides 2 inches high, and let rise till double. Bake in a hot oven over 15-20 minutes.

These are soft, fluffy rolls, fine for the tea-party type of luncheon.

Fruit rolls.—For a pleasant variation, roll the dough out in a sheet an inch thick and sprinkle thickly with 1 c chopped dates, 1 c chopped nuts, and 1 c chopped gumdrops (omit any flavors not liked). Roll as for jelly roll, and put in a greased loaf pan. Let rise till double in bulk. Bake in a hot oven 10 minutes and then in a moderate 20-30 more. Cool and slice in thick slices. Fine for breakfast or tea.

Makes 1 large roll.

Orange rolls.—Roll the dough in a sheet one-inch thick; spread with 6 T sugar and 1 grated orange rind that have been mixed and allowed to stand overnight, and dot with butter. Roll as jelly roll, and cut in 1-inch pieces. Place, just touching, on a greased pan with high sides, and let rise till double. Bake in a moderate oven about 15 minutes. Brush at once with a glaze made of:

GLAZE

¼ c light corn syrup	¼ c hot water
½ c sugar	1 T grated orange rind

Mix well.

Fine for a party, and the home folks will love them.

Makes about 3 dozen.

Mrs. A. S. Martin, Berea, Ohio

BUTTERHORN ROLLS

1 c scalded milk	2 cakes yeast
½ c sugar	2 T lukewarm water
1 t salt	½ t sugar
½ c shortening	4 c flour
3 well-beaten eggs	

Pour the milk over the next three ingredients following it. Cool and add the eggs. Add the yeast that has been mixed with the sugar and water; add the flour, using enough more for a soft dough that can be handled. Let rise till double in bulk.

Punch down, place on floured board, and knead about 5 minutes. Divide the dough in 3 parts. Roll each piece as nearly round as possible and about ¼-inch thick. Cut each into 16 pie-shaped pieces. Beginning at the broad end of the piece roll toward the small end. Put these pieces, curving the ends, on a greased baking sheet so that they will not touch. Let rise till double in bulk. Bake in a moderate oven about 25 minutes. Glaze, frost, or flavor as desired.

These are most attractive little horns that may be started at noon and be ready for dinner at six, please James!

Makes 3 dozen large or 4 dozen small rolls.

Mrs. Sylvia Kuechle, Cleveland, Ohio

BUTTERSCOTCH-PECAN ROLLS

2 cakes yeast	4¾ c flour
1 c milk, scalded and cooled	¼ c softened shortening
	1 t cinnamon
¼ c sugar	2 T butter
2 beaten eggs (or 4 egg yolks)	2 c B. sugar
	1 c broken nut meats
1 t salt	

Crumble the yeast in a bowl. Add the milk, and stir until the yeast dissolves. Add the next 5 ingredients in order. Knead well. Let rise till double in bulk. Punch down and let rise again till double. Roll out dough 1-inch thick on a floured board. Dot with the butter and ½ c of the B. sugar, and sprinkle with the cinnamon. Roll as for jelly roll. Cut in 1-inch pieces.

Place them just touching in a deep pan, the bottom of which is dotted with more butter and covered with the rest of the sugar and the nuts. Let rise till double and bake in a moderately hot oven about 30 minutes. Remove from the pan at once or the mixture will cause them to stick. These may be baked in muffin pans for individual rolls.

This is one of the most universally popular sweet rolls.

Philadelphia cinnamon or "sticky buns" may be made by using this same dough and method but sprinkling the sheet of dough thickly with currants and more cinnamon.

Makes about 3 dozen.

Mrs. Dorothy Lintner Pritchard, Columbus, Ohio

BUTTERMILK ROLLS

2 c buttermilk	2 T sugar
2 T shortening	1½ t salt
1 cake yeast	4–6 c flour
½ t soda	

Scald the milk, and pour it over the shortening. Cool, and add the rest, using only half the flour. Beat 3 minutes. Add the rest of the flour. Knead well on a floured board. Roll ½-inch thick. Brush with melted butter. Cut in rounds and place not touching on a greased pan with high sides. Let rise till double their size. Bake in a moderate oven 15-20 minutes. These are very tender because of the buttermilk.

Makes about 3 dozen.

Mrs. Ada Morgan Lintner, Linthaven Farm, Powell, Ohio

CARROT OR APPLE ROLLS

½ cake yeast	½ c cooked strained carrots
¼ c warm water	⅓ c cream (or evaporated
1 T sugar	milk)
¼ c shortening	1 beaten egg
¼ c sugar	1 t salt
	4-5 c flour

Mix the first 3 ingredients and let stand while you cream the shortening and sugar. Add the carrots, cream, egg, and salt. Combine the two mixtures and add the flour. Knead 2 minutes. Let rise till double in bulk. Punch down. Make rolls of any shape and place on a greased baking sheet to rise till double. Bake in a moderate oven 15-20 minutes.

This is a fine way to make children eat carrots, for they love these rolls. For apple rolls, omit the carrots and add 1 c chopped raw apple, substituting whole-wheat flour for half the white flour called for.

Makes 15 large rolls.

CORN ROLLS

1 c milk	1 cake yeast
¼ c sugar	¼ c warm water
1 t salt	2 beaten eggs
1 c corn meal	2 c flour
¼ c shortening	

Scald the milk, and add the next 4 ingredients. Cool. Mix the yeast with the water and add to the first mixture. Add eggs and flour. Knead, using more flour if necessary. Let rise till double in bulk. Punch down. Knead and roll 1-inch thick. Cut into rolls. Place on a greased deep pan not touching and let rise till twice their size. Bake in a hot oven 15-20 minutes.

For a variation, add 1 c chopped, dried fruit before rolling the dough.

These were called corn biscuit and considered a great delicacy served with hot chili after sleighing parties in the Pennsylvania hills where Mrs. Martin spent her girlhood.

Makes about 2 dozen.

Mrs. A. S. Martin, Berea, Ohio

DOUGHNUTS (Plain)

1¼ c milk, scalded and cooled to lukewarm	⅔ c sugar
1 cake yeast	½ t cinnamon
5½ c flour	½ t nutmeg
2 beaten eggs	2 T melted shortening
1 t salt	

Add the yeast to ¼ c of the milk. Stir till dissolved, and then add the rest of the milk. Add half the flour, mixing well. Add the rest in order and the rest of the flour. Knead on a floured board. Let rise till double in bulk. Punch down. Roll ¼-inch thick. Cut, and let rise on the board until almost double in size. Carefully put in deep fat, and fry till brown. Drain. Shake in a paper bag containing a mixture of G. sugar, or B. sugar and cinnamon.

If twists are preferred, twist together 4-inch ribbons of dough.

These are what five hungry children called "tough cruls" and enjoyed for the after-school piece.

Makes about 3 dozen.

Mrs. Ada Morgan Lintner, Linthaven Farm, Powell, Ohio

DOUGHNUTS (Refrigerator)

2 c milk	1 beaten egg
1½ c sugar	½ cake yeast
½ c shortening	½ c lukewarm water
¼ t each cinnamon and nutmeg	6-7 c flour
1 t salt	

Scald the milk, and add the next 4 ingredients. When the mixture is cool, add the egg, the yeast that has been softened in the water, and the flour. Let rise all night at room temperature. In the morning, punch down and roll out as much dough as desired for the first batch. Put the rest in a covered bowl in the refrigerator, where it can be kept about a week and used as desired. Cut the rolled dough in shapes or make into twists. Let rise on the board until double in bulk. Carefully put into hot, deep fat and fry till golden brown. Sugar as above.

This makes a fine recipe for those who like doughnuts, but not too many at once. For 2 people, half the recipe is ample. Makes 5-6 dozen.

Mrs. Dorothy Lintner Pritchard, Columbus, Ohio

HOT-CROSS BUNS

1 c milk	1 beaten egg
¼ c sugar	¼ c currants
3 T butter	2 T chopped citron
1 cake yeast	½ t nutmeg
¼ c warm water	½ t allspice
3-4 c flour	½ t cardamon
½ t salt	1 grated lemon rind

Scald the milk, add the sugar and butter, and cool. Soften the yeast in the water and set aside 5 minutes. Add this to the first mixture. Add the rest of the ingredients in order. Mix well. Let rise till double in bulk. Punch down and let rise again till double. Shape into flat, round buns and place on a deep, greased pan not touching. When they double their size, brush carefully with glaze of beaten egg yolk mixed with a little water. Sprinkle thickly with sugar. With a sharp knife, cut a cross. This sounds as if it would ruin the light bun, but it doesn't.

Bake in a hot oven about 30 minutes.

These buns may be frosted with a cross if a sweeter product is liked. For whole-wheat buns, substitute 1 c whole-wheat flour for 1 c of the white.

Hot-cross buns have a very ancient and honorable history. The Egyptians, the Greeks, the Saxons all made a crossed bun in honor of some goddess, believing that the cross had magic powers in preventing sickness or insuring good baking throughout the year. We associate the hot-cross bun with Easter time and the nursery jingle:

HOT-CROSS BUNS

"Hot-cross buns, hot-cross buns!
If you have no daughters,
Give them to your sons!"

Makes about 2 dozen.   *Mrs. Mary Lintner Lewis,* Rio Grande, Ohio

MAGIC BUTTER ROLLS

¼ c boiling water	2 cakes yeast
½ c butter	1 T sugar
¼ c undiluted, evaporated milk	3 c flour
	1 c finely chopped nuts
1 t salt	½ c sugar
3 beaten eggs	
1 t vanilla	

Pour the water over the butter. Cool. Add the milk, salt, eggs, vanilla, and the yeast which has been mixed with the T of sugar and let stand 10 minutes, and then add the flour. The dough will be stiff but slightly sticky. Let rise till double in bulk. Punch down. Cut pieces off dough with a spoon and roll in the nuts that have been mixed with the sugar. Twist each piece into a figure 8. Place on a greased baking sheet and let stand 10 minutes. Bake in a hot oven 10-15 minutes.

These are fine flavored, attractive, with a brown, crisp crust from the sugar-nut mixture. They are very good party rolls. Makes 2 dozen.

Mrs. Harriet Belt Loveless, Columbus, Ohio

MOM'S CINNAMON ROLLS WITH VARIATIONS

1 c unseasoned, warm mashed potatoes	½ c shortening
1 c warm potato water	½ c sugar
1 c scalded milk	2 t salt
1 cake yeast	2 beaten eggs
	6-7 c flour

Mix the first 3 ingredients. Cool. Add the crumbled yeast. Cream the shortening and sugar. Add the salt and eggs. Add this to the first mixture along with the flour, using enough more to make a stiff dough. Knead 1 minute. Let rise overnight. In the morning, roll a 1-inch-thick sheet, using more flour if necessary; sprinkle thickly with B. sugar and plenty of cinnamon. Roll as a jelly roll. Cut in inch pieces and place just touching on a deep-sided, greased pan. Let rise till double in bulk, and bake in a moderately hot oven 20-30 minutes. Glaze with C.

sugar and water mixed to a thin, spreading consistency.

These are fine for breakfast, for they may be kept several days and served hot or cold.

Cereal pinwheels.—Follow the same method, but sprinkle the sheet with Grape-Nuts or all bran and chopped dried fruits, or nuts if desired.

Fruit rolls or bread.—Add to the above dough this fruit mixture:

CINNAMON ROLLS

½ c ground, cooked, dried pears
½ c ground, cooked, dried prunes
½ c seedless raisins
⅛ c chopped citron
3 T chopped candied orange peel
¼ c chopped nuts
⅛ c sugar
1½ t cinnamon
⅛ t salt
1 egg white

If this is baked as a loaf, bake 10 minutes in hot oven and 50 more in moderate.

Sweet-potato rolls.—Substitute 1 c mashed sweet potato for the Irish potato and 1 c water for the potato water. Make these into attractive, yellow, pocketbook rolls.

Makes about 6 dozen.

Mrs. Alvin Zurcher, Chillicothe, Ohio

ONE-HOUR ROLLS

½ c milk
½ c water
4 T shortening
1 T sugar

1½ t salt
3 cakes yeast
⅓ c water
5-6 c flour

Scald the milk and add the next 4 ingredients. Cool.

Soften the yeast in the water and add it to the first mixture. Add the flour, and knead to form a good, firm dough. Knead

5 minutes more. Put in a warm place for 15 minutes. Punch down. Let rise for 10 more minutes. Punch down and make into rolls. Put on a greased baking sheet and let rise till double in size. Bake in a moderate oven 10-15 minutes.

These rolls depend for the quickness on the amount of yeast used and the temperature at which it is allowed to grow. About 88 degrees is the optimum, so, if your kitchen is not very warm, put them over a radiator or register, in a barely warm oven or in a pan of warm water. Be careful that the temperature does not run higher or the yeast will die and there'll be no rolls for dinner. If they should not rise as rapidly as scheduled, there is nothing wrong with the dough, but with the temperature. Makes about 3 dozen.

Laurabelle Ashbrook, Cleveland, Ohio

PLAIN RUSK

1 cake yeast	3 beaten eggs
¼ c lukewarm water	2½ c sugar
4 c milk, scalded and cooled	1 c melted shortening
	1 t nutmeg
16 cups flour	1 T salt

Soften the yeast in the water and add the milk and half the flour. Beat and let rise till very light and bubbly. Then add the rest of the ingredients and the remaining flour. Let rise till double in bulk. Knead down. Form smooth, round buns and place not touching on a greased baking sheet. Let rise till double in bulk and bake in a hot oven for 10 minutes and then in a moderate 15 minutes more.

This makes a huge quantity, but they are excellent toasted and buttered, or split and browned in a moderate oven.

The term rusk is used to apply to various light, sweet biscuits. In America they are usually served fresh, while in other countries they are made in loaves, sliced and rebaked, as for zwieback.

Mrs. Frank Stamats, Chillicothe, Ohio

ORANGE RUSK

⅓ c sugar
¼ c shortening
1 c strained orange juice
1 cake yeast
¼ c lukewarm water
1 beaten egg

¼ c finely chopped, candied
    orange peel
4 c flour
½ t nutmeg
1 t salt

Cream the sugar and shortening. Add the orange juice and the yeast softened in the water. Add the egg and peel and the dry ingredients. Mix well. Drop by teaspoonfuls in greased, tiny muffin tins. Let rise until double in size. Bake in a hot oven 10-15 minutes.

These have a wonderful flavor, color, and texture—just the thing for tea on a winter day, or for Sunday supper with a salad and hot chocolate. If there are any left, split and rebake them in moderate oven till brown and you have orange zwieback.

Makes about 4 dozen.

REFRIGERATOR ROLLS WITH VARIATIONS

1 c shortening
1 c sugar
1½ t salt
1 c boiling water

2 beaten eggs
2 cakes yeast
1 c cold water
6 c unsifted flour

Pour the boiling water over the shortening, sugar, and salt; blend and cool. Add the eggs. Let the yeast stand in the cold water five minutes. Mix, and add to the first mixture. Add the flour. Mix well. Let stand in a covered bowl in the refrigerator at least 4 hours before using; then it will keep a week to be used as wanted so that you may always have fresh rolls. Be sure the dough is in a large bowl, as it rises slightly in the refrigerator. About three hours before the rolls are wanted, make them into desired shapes, using more flour if necessary; but the dough should be soft, not toughened by too much flour. Place the rolls in a greased pan and let rise till double in bulk, about 2 hours. Bake in a hot oven 12-15 minutes. If a harder roll is liked, bake in a moderate oven about 20 minutes.

Variations in Shape

Bow-knot rolls. — Tie thin, long rounds of dough into bow knots.

Bread sticks. — Make long, ½-inch-thick rounds of dough. Glaze with egg, and sprinkle with Parmesan cheese.

Braided rolls. — Braid three long, thin strands of dough. Snip with scissors at the desired length. These are nice glazed with egg white or yolk and sprinkled with such seeds as poppy, sesame, or caraway.

Clover leaf. — Put 3 small balls of dough in muffin tins. Dip each ball in melted butter, if desired.

Crescents or horns. — Roll rounds of dough and cut in pie-shaped pieces. Roll from the outside in. Curve slightly at the ends and place an inch apart on the pan.

Crescent

Parker-house

Sticks

Twists

Clover Leaf

Braids

Plain

Pan Rolls

REFRIGERATOR-ROLL
VARIATIONS

Honey fingers.—Place twists in a pan, the bottom of which is covered with a half inch of honey and a thick sprinkle of chopped peanuts. Remove at once after baking.

Layer rolls.—Cut long, thin 2-inch-wide strips of dough. Brush with melted butter. Stack on similar strips till you have used six, cut about 3 inches long. Place in greased muffin tins with the cut ends up.

Pan rolls.—Place balls of dough almost touching, in deep-sided, square or round pans.

Parker House or Pocketbook rolls.—Cut rounds. Butter one side and fold the other over to form the pocketbook.

Twin rolls.—Put 2 small balls of dough in muffin tins. Dip each ball in melted butter if desired.

Twisted rolls.—Twist 2 thin strands of dough together and snip as braided rolls.

Variations in Ingredients

Bran rolls.—Add 1 c bran.

Cocoa.—Add 1 c cocoa and 1 extra egg.

Cheese rolls.—Add 2 c grated cheese.

Fruit rolls.—Add 2 c ground raisins, figs, dates, nuts, or any of these in combination, to the plain or the whole-wheat rolls.

Grape-Nuts.—Add 2 c Grape-Nuts.

Peanut butter.—Add 1 c peanut butter.

Rope-circle rolls.—Twist together 6-inch strips of white and whole-wheat dough, forming a circle and pinching the edges together.

Spice rolls.—Add 1 T of your favorite spice or any mixture of spices.

Toasted oats.—Toast ordinary, rolled oats in the oven and add 2 c of these to recipe.

Waffle loaf.—Weave together strips of dough to fit a square tin. When this rises it will look like the grids of a waffle iron on top.

Whole-wheat rolls.—Substitute 3 c whole-wheat flour for 3 c of white.

FILLINGS FOR PINWHEEL ROLLS

Cocktail rolls.—Roll out a sheet of dough and spread with anchovy paste, chutney, mustard, snappy cheese spread, fish flakes, ground, baked ham, or any savory filling. Roll as jelly roll. Cut in tiny rounds.

Fruit-and-nut rolls.—Make as above, using currants, dates, ground figs or prunes, nuts, candied peel, grated rind, conserve, marmalade, peanut butter, or any combination of these. Fine for breakfast, luncheon, or tea.

SURPRISES

Use thin sheets of dough to cover the "surprise," which may be an orange, tangerine, or grapefruit section, a date, pitted and stuffed with a nut, a fig, apricot, or prune stuffed with a bit of marshmallow. Use your imagination and produce a real tea dainty. This same surprise may be achieved by putting a bit of dough in the bottom of a muffin tin, then the filling, and then covering the top with dough.

If you are in a hurry, this dough may be used as the basis of any type of roll you want to make. It is a rich dough and will stand for a good bit of abuse. Therefore it is excellent for beginners in yeast to play with. If you want to make butterscotch rolls and are afraid of the recipe, use this. We have never known of a failure with this dough if the simple directions are followed. It is fun to see how many different kinds of rolls you can make from one batch of dough.

Makes about 5 dozen.

SOUR-CREAM COFFEE ROLLS

2 c milk
1 c sour cream
¾ c shortening
1 t salt
1 c sugar

4 beaten eggs
2 cakes yeast
¼ c warm water
13 c flour

Scald the milk and cream. Add the shortening, salt, and sugar, and cool. Add the eggs and the yeast that has been softened in the water. Add the flour for a stiff dough. Blend well. Let rise till double in bulk. Punch down. Cover the bottom of large muffin tins with ½-inch-thick pieces of dough. Cover with filling, and put another piece of dough on top. This may be baked as a coffee loaf in the same manner, covering the bottom of a loaf pan with dough, putting in the filling, and then covering the filling, sandwich fashion. Let rise till double in bulk. Bake *rolls* in a hot oven about 25 minutes—bread, in a hot oven 10 minutes and then in a moderate 40 more.

FILLING

1 c cooked, chopped
  prunes
½ c sugar

½ c chopped nuts
1 t cinnamon
⅓ c raisins

This is very tender and well flavored.

Makes 3 large loaves and about 8 dozen rolls.

SURPRISE ROLLS

1 cake yeast
¼ c warm water
1 T sugar
⅓ c cream
½ c milk
1 T shortening

½ c sugar
½ t salt
⅓ c cooked, strained pumpkin, squash, or sweet potato
1 beaten egg
5-6 c flour

Mix the first 3 ingredients and let stand 10 minutes. Scald the cream and milk and add shortening, sugar, salt, and potato. Cool. Add the egg, the yeast mixture, and the flour. Let rise till double in bulk. Punch down. Roll 1-inch-thick sheet, dot with butter, and sprinkle with B. sugar and cinnamon, graham cracker crumbs, date slices, and bits of marshmallow. Roll as jelly roll and place in a circle on a round, greased pan. Pinch the edges together; with scissors cut half through the roll at 2-inch intervals. Let rise till double in bulk. Bake in a moderate oven 45-50 minutes. Brush with melted butter.

Fine hot or cold for tea or Sunday supper, because of its most unusual flavor.

Makes 2 rolls.

WHITE HORNS

1 cake yeast	4 beaten egg yolks
2 T lukewarm water	3/4 t salt
3/4 c cream	3-3 1/2 c flour
3/4 c shortening	

Crumble the yeast in the water, and let stand 5 minutes. Scald the cream and add the shortening. Cool. Add the yeast mixture and the rest of the ingredients in order. This may be mixed in an electric mixer with unbeaten egg yolks. Put the dough in a wet napkin, tied at the top. Place it in a bowl and cover it with water of room temperature or as it comes from the tap at the start. Let it stand until the dough floats, about 2 hours. Turn it out on a plate. Drop by teaspoon into the topping, and shape into small horns. Place on greased baking sheet so that they do not touch. Let rise till double in bulk, and bake in a moderate oven 15-20 minutes.

TOPPING

1 c sugar	1/2 c finely chopped, blanched
1 t cinnamon	almonds

These are deliciously light and different.

Makes 2-3 dozen.

Mrs. Laura Seefried Horsfall, Avon Lake, Ohio

Pancakes, Raised

BUCKWHEAT CAKES

1/3 c flour, corn meal, or bread crumbs	1/4 cake yeast
2 c scalded milk	1/3 c lukewarm water
2/3 t salt	2 T Orleans molasses or
1 1/4 c buckwheat flour	B. sugar
	1/4 t soda

Soak the flour, meal, or crumbs in the milk until it is cool. Add the salt and flour. Add the yeast softened in the water. Put in a covered bowl or pitcher and let rise all night. In the morning add the remaining ingredients and blend well. Bake and serve hot.

This is known as the Good Old-fashioned Buckwheat Cake with a capital letter. In the Lintner home, when real cold weather, sausage cakes, and maple syrup came, a batch was set in an old stone pitcher large enough so that the batter wouldn't "rise all over the floor," a part of it to be saved after each baking for a starter and replenished with more of each ingredient except the yeast, as the starter took care of the leavening agent. Tradition demanded that the cakes be made very thin and the full size of the griddle, making them about 8 inches in diameter. There's no pancake with a flavor like these, but if you're not used to it you will have to cultivate a liking for the sour, yeasty taste.

Makes 6 large cakes.

Mrs. Ada Morgan Lintner, Linthaven Farm, Powell, Ohio

CORN GRIDDLECAKES

1 c corn meal	1 cake yeast
2 c boiling water	2 T warm water
2 c flour	2 beaten eggs
1 T B. sugar	1/4 t B.P.
2 c milk, scalded and cooled	1 1/2 t salt

Pour the boiling water over the meal. Beat well and cool to lukewarm. Add the flour, sugar, milk, and yeast mixed with the water. Let stand all night. In the morning add the rest of the ingredients with more corn meal if necessary for a pour batter (about 1⅓ c). Mix well and bake. As with buckwheat cakes, save about 1 c of batter for a starter and continue "starting" till your taste for these good cakes vanishes.
Makes about 2 dozen.

Mrs. Frank Stamats, Chillicothe, Ohio

Sourdough

Frontiersmen are known as Sourdoughs because they make a pancake or biscuit out of "Sourdough" made in the manner of Salt Rising Bread, using the wild yeast from the air. Each day they save part of the dough as a "starter" or "leaven" for the next day's batch. To this they add more flour, salt, water, or milk and occasionally an egg or a little soda, if the dough is too sour. This is an endless process as long as the starter "works."

If you want to try it, follow the directions for Salt Rising Bread, p. 92, using only enough flour for a pour batter for pancakes, and enough to roll for biscuits. Wild yeast is precarious; therefore no results are guaranteed.

WAFFLES (Raised)

½ yeast cake	1 c milk
3 T lukewarm water	2 c flour
1 beaten egg	½ t salt
1½ t melted butter	

Mix the yeast and water, and let stand in a warm place ½ hour. Add the rest in order given. These may be baked at once, or it will not hurt them to stand a bit. They have that good yeast flavor and the added advantage of being very crisp.
Serves 6.

Mrs. Fern McCann, Gahanna, Ohio

AUSTRIA

Some one has said that the breads of Austria add to "Gemütlichkeit," or the joy of living. Certain it is that the famous Vienna bread has made its way all over the world to achieve a popularity that is well deserved in spite of the fact that it has had to allow all sorts of unworthy imitations to be sold under its name; and in spite of the fact that some heretics claim there is no Vienna bread, saying that it is just a name given to "pain riche" and never had a thing to do with Vienna. Skeptics to the contrary notwithstanding, there once was a group of famous gourmets who pronounced Vienna bread the best in the world and advised that it be eaten fresh.

But Austria has more to offer than Vienna bread. From a batch of delightfully fluffy yeast dough, some caraway, and poppy seeds, one can toss up such delicacies as kipfel (breakfast crescents) or krapfen (doughnuts). Then, with a very special yeast dough plus many almonds and some fruit, one evolves the kugelhupf, a delicate cakelike bread that is just right with afternoon coffee and yet is so good that one is tempted to save it for the evening dessert!

KIPFEL (Rolls)

1 c milk	1 cake yeast
2 T butter	1/4 c lukewarm water
1 t salt	4 c flour
1 T sugar	

Scald the milk and add the butter, salt, and sugar. Cool. Soften the yeast in the water and add. Add the flour and knead well 1 minute. Let rise till double in bulk. Roll 1/2-inch thick, and cut in 3-cornered pieces. Spread with butter and roll the large end toward the small. Shape in horns. Place on a greased baking sheet an inch apart and brush with melted butter. Let rise till double in size. Bake in a hot oven 15-20 minutes.

KIPFEL

If these are mixed at noon they are ready for dinner, and are excellent with that meal, as they are not sweet. They are also an excellent breakfast roll with a delicious buttery crust.
Makes 3 dozen.

KRAPFEN (Crullers)

1/4 c sugar	1/2 c sour cream
1/2 t salt	2 c flour
4 egg yolks	1 grated lemon rind
1/2 c wine or	

Mix the sugar, salt, and egg yolks. Beat well. Add the liquid, the flour, and the lemon rind, and mix to a smooth dough. Roll out thin and cut in shape of a playing card. Make 2 incisions and pull one corner through each incision making it look like a screw. Fry in hot fat till brown. Sugar and serve at once. This is like a rich cracker.
Makes about 2 dozen.

KUGELHUPF

1¼ c milk	4 beaten egg yolks
¼ c shortening	4½ c flour
½ c sugar	¾ c chopped raisins
½ t salt	2 egg whites, stiffly beaten
1 cake yeast	⅓ c blanched almond halves
1 grated lemon rind	

KUGELHUPF

Scald the milk, and add the shortening, sugar, and salt. Cool. Add the crumbled yeast and the rest of the ingredients in order except the almonds. Mix well. Put in a greased tube pan with the almonds in the bottom. Let rise till double in bulk. Bake in a hot oven 10 minutes and then in a moderate 50-60 more. Remove and sprinkle with C. sugar.

This is a great delicacy served hot or cold with afternoon coffee or for dessert.

Makes 1 large loaf.

VIENNA BREAD

2 cakes yeast	1 c water
1 T sugar	8 c flour
¼ c water	1 T salt
1 c milk, scalded and cooled	

Mix the first 3 and let stand till bubbly. Add the rest in order and let rise till double in bulk. Punch down. Knead. Let rise till double in bulk. Punch down and knead very well. Shape into long thin loaves. With scissors, make gashes in the top of the loaf, about 3 inches apart and ½-inch deep. Let rise, not touching, on a greased baking sheet until double in bulk. Carefully brush with slightly beaten egg white. Bake in a hot oven 10 minutes and then in a moderate 50 more. Remove from the oven. Brush well with egg white and sprinkle with salt and poppy or sesame seeds. Return to the moderate oven for 30 minutes more or until the seeds are brown.

This is a delicious bread with a crisp, good crust.

Makes 2 large loaves.

VIENNA TARTS

½ c cottage cheese	1 c flour
½ c butter	¼ t salt

Cut the butter and cheese into the flour and salt as for piecrust. Chill ½ hour. Roll thin. Cut in squares. Put a spoonful of jam or jelly in the middle and pinch all the edges together to hold the filling. Bake in a hot oven 10 minutes or until brown.

These are very rich but mighty good.

With a highly seasoned meat filling they are good in small shapes with beer or cocktails. They may be made in the morning, kept in the icebox, and baked just before the party.

Makes about 6.

CZECHOSLOVAKIA

This country that has been so torn apart has managed, through all her trials, to preserve a taste for good bread. As one woman said, "We grow good grain in our country, so we have good flour, and good flour makes good bread." She went on to say that they were fond of rye, the light variety, "with or without seeds, it makes no difference to us at all." These people seem to know what to do with their good flour, for they make very good bread. The fancy kinds are not so eggy and rich as the Hungarian, for instance; nor so light and delightfully puffy as the Scandinavian, but they are well flavored and substantial without being the least bit heavy. The Czechs seem to be fond of poking holes in various shapes of yeast dough and filling those holes with marmalade, bits of dried fruit, or cheese. They like the horn and crescent shapes too, all filled with poppy seeds or nuts.

BRAIDED FRUIT BREAD

1 cake yeast
¼ c lukewarm water
1 beaten egg
½ c sugar
⅓ c melted shortening
2 c milk, scalded and
 cooled

½ t salt
½ c chopped raisins
½ c chopped citron
½ c chopped, blanched
 almonds
8-10 c flour

Add the water to the yeast and set aside. Mix the egg, sugar, shortening, milk, and salt, and 2 c of the flour. Add to yeast mixture. Let rise 1 hour. Add the rest of the flour and the fruits and nuts. Knead well using more flour if necessary. Let rise till double in bulk. Divide the dough in 3 unequal parts. Divide each of those parts in 3 and braid so that you have 3 braids. Place the braids on top of each other, the smallest on top, on a greased baking sheet. Let rise till double in bulk. Bake in a hot oven 10 minutes and a moderate about 40 more. Ice when cool with C. sugar and water mixed to a paste or brush with slightly beaten egg white while still warm.

Here is a delicious bread, full of fruit and different to look at. Makes 1 huge loaf.

KOLACKY (Little Cakes) WITH VARIATIONS

1 c shortening
4 c flour
1 t salt
4 beaten egg yolks
1 c warm cream

¼ c sugar
1 grated lemon rind
1 cake yeast
1 T warm water
½ t sugar

Mix the shortening, flour, and salt as for pie dough. Add the eggs, cream, sugar, and lemon rind. Add the yeast mixed with the water and sugar. Mix well. Let rise till double in bulk. Roll out on a heavily floured board to ½-inch thickness. Cut in rounds with a large cookie cutter. Press on top of each a pitted prune or apricot that has been soaked until plump, or a spoonful of cottage cheese, or stiff marmalade. Brush with slightly beaten egg white and sprinkle with sugar. Let rise on a greased baking sheet placed so that they do not touch, until double in size, or they may be made in muffin tins. Bake in a hot oven about 15-20 minutes.

These are very rich, but deliciously tender; fine for afternoon coffee.

This word has various spellings as Kolatchen, Kolace, Kolashes.

Sour Cream Kolacky.—Use 1 c sour cream for the cream called for.

Spice Kolacky.—Add 2 t cinnamon, 1 t mace, and 1 t anise seed. Put a fat raisin in the center of each round; spread with egg yolk mixed with water and sprinkle well with sugar and cinnamon.

Sugar Circles.—Make the center depression very deep and fill it with a bit of melted butter and much B. sugar.

Makes about 3 dozen.

Mrs. Mary Piter, Cleveland, Ohio

MARMALADE KUCHEN

1 c milk	1 cake yeast
¼ c sugar	2 T lukewarm water
1 t salt	1 beaten egg
¼ c shortening	4 c flour

Scald the milk and add the next 3 ingredients. Cool. Soften the yeast in the water and add. Add the egg and flour and blend well. Knead until smooth. Put in long, well greased, shallow pan. Spread with softened butter and let rise till double in bulk. Then with the floured handle of a wooden spoon, or a floured thumb will do, make holes in the kuchen at 2-inch intervals all over. Fill these with orange marmalade and bake in a hot oven about 35 minutes.

This is interesting to look at, but more interesting to eat, with a big cup of good coffee.

Makes 1 large kuchen.

Mrs. Mary Piter, Cleveland, Ohio

POPPY SEED CRESCENTS

FILLING

2 c water
1 c sugar
1 c ground poppy seeds

½ t cinnamon
1 t grated lemon rind

Boil the sugar and water until a thick syrup is formed. Add the rest and cool. Using the marmalade kuchen dough, roll out a ½ inch sheet. Cut in triangles and spread each with filling. Roll the large end toward the small to make crescents. Curve the ends. Place not touching on a greased baking sheet and brush with egg yolk mixed with water. Sprinkle with sugar and finely ground nuts and let rise till double in bulk. Bake in a hot oven about 20 minutes.

Mrs. Piter says that the Czechoslovakian people are very fond of the poppy seed flavor; learn to enjoy it if you're to appreciate this delicacy.

Makes about 2 dozen.

Mrs. Mary Piter, Cleveland, Ohio

POPPY SEED ROLL

¼ c C. sugar
2 T butter (sweet if possible)
1 beaten egg
¼ t salt

¼ cake yeast
1 T lukewarm water
¼ c lukewarm cream
2 c flour

FILLING

1 c ground poppy seeds mixed with honey and milk to form stiff paste.

Cream the sugar and butter. Add the egg and salt and beat well. Add the yeast mixed with the water. Add the cream. Add 1 c of the flour and beat well. Add the rest of the flour to make a stiff dough. Let rise over

POPPY SEED ROLL

night. In the morning roll ½-inch thick and spread with filling or nuts. Roll as jelly roll and place on a greased cookie sheet. Let rise till double in bulk and bake in a hot oven 10 minutes and a moderate 50 more.

The poppy seed filling is characteristic of much Czechoslovakian baked goods. The ground poppy seeds have an odd flavor, the taste for which must be cultivated. Use ground nuts if liked better.

Makes 1 roll.

Mrs. Mary Piter, Cleveland, Ohio

TRICORNS

2 c milk
½ c shortening
½ c sugar
1 t salt
1 t nutmeg
1 cake yeast

¼ c water
2 beaten eggs
6 c unsifted flour
(more if necessary in kneading)

Scald the milk and add the next four ingredients. Cool. Add the yeast which has been softened in the water. Add the eggs and flour. Blend. Let rise until double in bulk. Punch down and knead well. Roll thin. Cut in rounds. Put a spoonful of filling in the center and pinch up the edges to look like a tricorn. Place on a greased cookie sheet and let rise till double in bulk. Sprinkle with sugar. Bake in a moderate oven about 25 minutes.

Use any of the fillings on p. 177 or any kind of stiff marmalade or jam.

Makes 4-5 dozen.

ENGLAND

What with London having a Bread Street, where Milton was born, it is no wonder that good English breads and literature have long enjoyed a close friendship. Many of us owe to our reading of English novels our first acquaintance with such delicacies as muffins and crumpets, Bath buns (than which there is nothing better), saffron bread all full of caraway seeds and maybe a bit of rose water, holiday fruit breads, thin bread and butter for tea—the bread world would indeed be a sorry place without all those good things from England.

American people find it very easy to like English breads, for, as Florence White points out in *Good Things from England*,* "Our kitchen has more in common with America than with any other country. This is natural, as the foundations of both the English and American kitchen were the same up to 1630; England is proud of the national kitchen American women have developed on their own individual lines, and one of the interests of this direct research . . .

---

* White, Florence, *Good Things from England*. Jonathan Cape, London.

has been to come across continual evidence of our common family interests with our cousins across the Atlantic."

English bakeshops turn out excellent products, but, even with the English themselves, there seems to be a nostalgic longing for the homemade. Lady Raglan, in her memoirs, speaking of a house party, says, "Everything was homemade, the bread and the cakes and the scones." As Miss White says, "There is no reason, however, why we should not make some bread and scones at home for a treat, even if we live in a small town flat, or in the country where we can have only an oil stove with an oven; or merely a girdle over a wood fire made on a hearth out of doors. . . ." Since it is impossible for us ever to have the bakeshop products, we must follow Miss White's advice and turn to the kitchen. Be assured it will not be a hardship but a pleasure to turn out a real Bath bun or a crusty loaf. After all, the Anglo-Saxon word "hlæfdige," or "loaf-giver," became our word lady.

Bath Buns

These were originated in Bath, England, whence their fame has spread not only all over England, but all over this country as well. This is an old recipe, not to be made, as it is a bit uncertain, but to be read for pure enjoyment. It makes an interesting contrast to the more modern recipes.

BATH CAKES VERY GOOD

"Take one-half ap^{nd} of fine flour take of Sack and ale yest each six Spoonfulls and of rose water and 7 egg whites

and all Mix these together set it by ye fire to rise while it is rising take ap^nd of flour and ap^nd of butter and Mix well together and put in ap^nd of Carroway Comfets Just before you make them up Butter your papers and put a Spoonful for a cake this will make six dozen."

BATH BUNS (Old-Fashioned)

2 c shortening	1 T sherry
4 c flour	1 T rose water
¾ c sugar	8 beaten eggs
1 cake yeast	2 T caraway comfits (seeds)

Work together the shortening, 2 c of the flour, and the sugar. Soften the yeast in the sherry and rose water. Add the other 2 c of flour and the eggs. Let this rise 2 hours. Then work in the first mixture, and add half the caraway seeds. Drop large spoons of dough on a greased baking sheet, and sprinkle the tops with caraway seed. Let rise ½ hour, and bake in a moderately hot oven 20-30 minutes.

This is an 18th-century recipe that is still used in some places. It has not been dressed up with all the fruit which is in the modern recipes. Modern people may add ½ t salt.

Makes about 2 dozen.

Margaret J. Brown, Cleveland, Ohio

BATH BUNS (Modern)

1 cake yeast	⅓ c sugar
½ c milk, scalded and cooled	1 c chopped almonds
1 T sugar	¼ c chopped citron or orange peel
½ c butter	½ c currants
4 beaten eggs	½ c chopped raisins
4 c flour	6 candied cherries
½ t salt	

Crumble the yeast in a bowl. Add the milk and sugar, and mix well. Add the butter and eggs, flour and salt. Mix well. This will be stiff but not enough to handle. Let it rise until very light, more than double in bulk. Punch down and add the rest of the ingredients. Work well with a spoon. Drop large spoons of dough on a greased baking sheet. These buns should be rather flat and rough on top from the fruit. Do not attempt to smooth them out. Let them rise ½ hour, and then bake in a moderately hot oven 15-20 minutes. Remove them from the oven and glaze with 1 beaten egg yolk mixed with 1 T water. Sprinkle thickly with crushed loaf sugar and return to the oven for 1 minute.

Bath Buns are one of the most appetizing of breakfast breads. In some families they have been a Sunday morning tradition for years.

Makes about 2 dozen.

Mrs. Mary Lou Bradfield Brasseur, Cleveland, Ohio

CORNISH SEEDY BREAD

To the recipe for Cornish Yeasty Splits (below) add 6 T melted shortening and 1 T caraway seeds. Mix well. Let rise till double in bulk. Shape into loaves and let rise in a greased shallow pan 30 minutes. Bake in a hot oven 30-40 minutes.

Makes 2 loaves.

Bockes and Cochran, Cleveland, Ohio

CORNISH SPLITS

2 c flour	2 t B.P.
½ t salt	¾ c buttermilk

Mix to a biscuitlike dough. Roll out ½ inch thick. Cut in rounds and bake in a hot oven about 10 minutes.

These are very much like our biscuits, but not so rich since they depend only on the buttermilk to make them tender. They should be split as the name suggests and served with lots of butter and jam.

Makes about 1 dozen.

Bockes and Cochran, Cleveland, Ohio

CORNISH YEASTY SPLITS

½ cake yeast
1 T sugar
1 c milk, scalded and
  cooled

2 T melted butter
4 c flour
½ t salt

Cream the yeast and sugar until liquified. Add the milk, the butter, and the dry ingredients. Work into a smooth dough and let rise in a "basin," as the English say, until double in bulk. Knead again and shape into small round cakes. Let them rise on a greased baking sheet until double in bulk, and bake in a hot oven 15-20 minutes. For a richer "split," double the amount of butter.

These may be split and served hot or cold, with plenty of butter, jam, or treacle (syrup to us). If eaten with treacle and cream they are called Thunder and Lightning.

Makes about 2 dozen.

Bockes and Cochran, Cleveland, Ohio

CRUMPETS

Use the English muffin recipe (p. 129) with 2 c less flour. This makes a batter. Let it rise 3 times, 30 minutes each time, beating 3-4 minutes between each rising. This beating makes the large holes, characteristic of the crumpet. After the last beating, bake at once by pouring the batter into muffin rings set on a hot, greased griddle. Fill the rings ⅓ full and let them bake about 20 minutes. Do not turn. Let cool. Toast and serve with butter and jam.

A crumpet is like a muffin but larger (about 3¼ inches) and thinner. They are full of holes, and some people call them "plain soggy," while others say that is the way they should be and eat them with a relish. One person of the former opinion has called them "a blanket soaked in butter."

Makes about 1 dozen.

CHRISTMAS BREAD

1⅓ c boiling water	¼ t nutmeg
¼ c lard	1 c currants
¼ c butter	¾ c raisins
2 t salt	½ c chopped citron
½ c sugar	1 t caraway (optional)
2 cakes yeast	1 t allspice
¼ c lukewarm water	6 c flour
1 T sugar	

Pour the boiling water over the next 4 ingredients. When it is lukewarm, add the yeast cakes that have been softened in the water and the 1 T sugar. Add all the rest and knead well. Let rise all night; it takes a long time because of all the fruit. In the morning knead again and put in greased loaf pans (round are good) and let rise till double in bulk. Bake in a hot oven 10 minutes and a moderately slow 100 more.

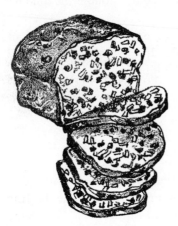

CHRISTMAS BREAD

Because this bread keeps well it is excellent to have all through the holiday season. There is an old tradition that if the bread is baked on Christmas Eve it will never mold. Another tradition says that if part of a loaf is allowed to remain on the table after the Christmas Eve dinner, there will never be a lack of bread in the home for the next year.

Makes 2 large loaves.

Mrs. Ada Morgan Lintner, Linthaven Farm, Powell, Ohio

DERBYSHIRE OAT CAKE

5⅓ c steel-cut or ground, rolled oats	1 t salt
4 c warm water	½ cake yeast

Mix, crumbling the yeast in last. Let it rise 2 hours. Beat well (it is a thin batter) and pour 1 c of batter on a well-greased, heavy frying pan. Let it cook slowly till brown on the bottom; turn and brown on the other side.

These will be damp and limp at first, but must be dried out. The old way was to hang them across a pole or clothesline and toast them before the fire just before eating. Modern cooks crisp them in the oven. These have a slightly bitter taste and a coarse texture. They are good with cheese for those who have cultivated a liking for them.

Makes about 6 dozen.

DORSET APPLE CAKE

1 c flour
½ c sugar
1 t B.P.
⅛ t salt

½ c dripping (any shortening)
1 c finely chopped raw apple
1 T milk

Mix the first 4 ingredients and cut in the shortening. Add the apples and milk, using more milk if the apples are not juicy. Mix into a flat, round cake. Bake on a greased pan in a moderate oven about 30 minutes.

Good, but rich. Gooseberries or currants may be substituted for the apple and will give a flavor and variety of their own to this old favorite.

DORSET APPLE CAKE

This is served hot for tea with lots of butter and cream if desired.

Leftover portions may be reheated.

Makes 1 cake.

DEVONSHIRE POTATO CAKE

2 c flour	¾ c dripping (any shorten-
¼ c sugar	ing)
¼ t salt	1½ c mashed potatoes
⅓ c currants	1 beaten egg

Mix in order. Roll ⅓-inch thick. Cut in rounds. Bake on a slightly greased griddle over a low flame until brown on both sides, or bake in a moderate oven 15 minutes.

Serve these hot for tea, especially with a "fruit tea" if the fruit is strawberries and if there is plenty of clotted cream. This tea dish is a delicacy peculiar to Devonshire. It is made by heating whole milk, cooking it, and taking off the thick layers of cream as they rise to the top. It is used on fruit or as a spread in place of butter.

Makes about 2 dozen.

GIPSY SPICE BREAD

4 c flour	1 t ginger
1¼ c B. sugar	1 c black treacle (Orleans
1⅓ c sultana raisins	molasses)
¼ c grated peel	3 beaten eggs
½ t allspice	¾ c milk
	1 t soda

Mix the first 6 ingredients. Add the rest, with the soda dissolved in the milk. Mix well. Put in greased loaf pans and bake in a slow oven about 2 hours.

This is a solid, fruity, flavorful bread that keeps well. It is fine to have around for children's pieces.

Makes 2 loaves.

Mrs. Ada Morgan Lintner, Linthaven Farm, Powell, Ohio

MORGAN FINE WHITE BREAD WITH VARIATION

2 c milk	1 cake yeast
¼ c shortening	1 t sugar
1 T salt	¼ c lukewarm milk
1 beaten egg	8 c flour

Scald the milk; add the shortening and salt. Cool. Add the beaten egg and the yeast mixed with the sugar and milk. Add the flour. Knead well. Let rise till double in bulk. Knead again and shape into loaves. These are the manchet of olden times. Let rise close together on a greased baking sheet until double in bulk. Bake in a hot oven 10 minutes and a moderate 50 more.

Fruit bread.—Add 2 cups of any kind of chopped dried fruit or nuts before shaping the loaves. This may be made in small forms for breakfast or tea. Currant and raisin bread were two very special treats of the Lintner home.

Makes 2 loaves.

Mrs. Ada Morgan Lintner, Linthaven Farm, Powell, Ohio

MUFFINS (Old Fashioned)

10 c flour	1 T salt
1¼ c milk	½ T sugar
2 c water	1 cake yeast

Mix all, and add the yeast softened in the sugar last. Mix well. Let rise till double in bulk. Mix again. Put a lot of flour on a board and make 3-inch holes at intervals. Fill these holes with dough ½-inch thick. Let the muffins rise twice their size and carefully slip them with a spatula onto a greased, heavy griddle, putting the upper side down on the griddle. Bake them over a low flame (an asbestos mat under the griddle helps keep them

ENGLISH MUFFINS

an even temperature) until they are brown on one side (about 15 minutes). Turn and bake on the other. Muffins may be baked in rings as crumpets (see p. 125), or they may be rolled and cut instead of shaped in the flour holes, but extra flour for kneading must be added.

These may be served at once or cooled and toasted. Most Americans cut them in two parts and toast both sides, but the English say this makes them tough. The proper way is to tear them around the outer edge, "Scotch them round the waist," as they say, and toast on both sides on a fork over a fire, then break them open and serve with lots of butter and bitter orange marmalade for tea.

Notice that the English Muffin is in no way related to the American variety.

Makes about 2 dozen.

Juanita B. Jones, Cleveland, Ohio

MUFFINS (Modern Refrigerator Method)

1 cake yeast	2 T butter
½ c lukewarm water	1 t salt
1 c milk	4-5 c flour

Soften the yeast in the water. Add the butter and salt to the scalded milk. Cool, and add the yeast mixture and 2 c of the flour. Beat until smooth. Let rise 1 hour, then add the rest of the flour and knead until smooth. Let rise till double in bulk. This may be used at once or kept in the refrigerator until needed. Don't keep longer than a week. Follow the baking instructions given above.

These are delicious with a salad luncheon. For a richer or "Chester Muffin" add ½ c sugar, ½ c melted butter, and 2 beaten eggs.

The muffin man's bell was one of the interesting sounds of earlier times. Everybody remembers the nursery rhyme about it.

Makes about 1 dozen.

Juanita B. Jones, Cleveland, Ohio

PARKIN

2 c steel-cut or ground, rolled oats	½ t ginger
	¼ t mace
2 c flour	1 c shortening
½ t salt	1 T cream
1 t B.P.	½ c black treacle (Orleans molasses)
1 t soda	
¼ t nutmeg	

Mix the first 8 ingredients. Cut in the shortening. Add the rest in order, to form a stiff dough. Let stand all night. In the morning put in a shallow greased pan and bake in a moderate oven 1 hour. 1 c candied, chopped peel may be added for a variation.

This will keep well in a covered crock or cookie jar, and will improve with age. Parkin is really the English version of gingerbread. It is not to be judged by our standards of gingerbread, for it is a solid loaf, good for munching and children's pieces.

Makes 2 medium loaves.

PLAIN PARKIN

4 c flour	2 t ginger
1 c sugar	½ c shortening (melted)
1 t soda	1 beaten egg
2 t B.P.	1 c treacle (Orleans
¼ t salt	molasses)
	2 c milk

Mix in order. Put in greased loaf pans and bake in a moderate oven about 1 hour. This recipe was brought from England by Mrs. H. Hanson.

Makes 2 medium loaves.

Mrs. H. Hanson, Kirkwood, Missouri

RICE BREAD

½ cake yeast	1 c flour
¼ c lukewarm water	½ c cooked rice
1 t sugar	½ t salt

Mix the yeast, water, and sugar. Add the rest and knead, using more flour if the dough is too sticky to handle. Let rise till double in bulk. Shape into loaves and let rise again until double in bulk. Bake in a moderate oven 1 hour.

Very good flavor.

Makes 1 small loaf.

RUSK (Quick)

2 c flour	½ c shortening
¼ t salt	1 beaten egg
2 t B.P.	¼ c milk

Mix in order, cutting the shortening in. Form stiff dough and roll out. Cut in rounds and bake on a greased baking sheet in a hot oven 15 minutes. Break apart; return to the oven, rough side up, till brown.

Serve at once, with butter and jam, for tea.

Makes about 1 dozen.

Mrs. Betty Goode Sprague, Cleveland, Ohio

RUSK (Yeast)

½ cake yeast	2 T butter
2 T sugar	½ t salt
1 T warm water	1 beaten egg
1 c milk	3 c flour

Mix the yeast, sugar, and water. Scald the milk and add the butter and salt. When it is cool, add the yeast mixture, the egg, and the flour. Knead. Let rise till double. Knead again and shape into a long loaf. Let rise till double in bulk. Bake in a greased pan in a hot oven 10 minutes and a moderate 40 more.

English rusk is made in this loaf shape, cooled, sliced thick, and the slices dried and browned in a moderately slow oven —like zwieback.

Makes about 1 dozen.

SALLY LUNN

1 cake yeast	½ t salt
1 c rich cream or evap-	2 beaten eggs
orated milk	1 c butter (to spread on
4 c flour	the bread)

Mix the yeast, cream, and half the flour. Let rise 1 hour. Add the rest of the flour and the remaining ingredients. Let rise till double in bulk. Knead. Put in a greased loaf pan and let rise again till double in size. Bake in a hot oven 10 minutes and a moderate 40 more.

Authorities seem to differ about how this bread should be served. Some say to tear it apart lengthwise, "scotch it round the waist," butter it generously, and return the halves to the oven until all the butter has melted into the loaf. Others say it is never correct to use butter; rich, thick cream is the only thing. Others use it with ordinary amounts of butter as one would a very good, home-baked loaf. Take your choice.

"Sally Lunn" was first made by a young woman of that name who lived in Lilliput Alley, Bath, England, during the 18th century. She is said to have catered for the famous

SALLY LUNN

Beau Nash's parties, and therefore must have been one of the best pastry cooks of her time. Her shop was rediscovered and reopened not many years ago and serves the famous "Sally Lunn" made according to the lady's own recipe.

Makes 2 medium loaves.

Juanita B. Jones, Cleveland, Ohio

SAFFRON BREAD

½ t saffron	2 T butter
1⅔ c boiling water	2 t salt
2 cakes yeast	10-12 c flour
¼ c sugar	2 c currants
1⅔ c evaporated milk	½ c chopped citron

Pour the water over the saffron, steep 5 minutes, strain, and cool. Mix the sugar and yeast. Scald the milk and add the butter and salt. Cool. Combine these mixtures and add the rest. Mix well and knead. Let rise till double in bulk. Knead again and let rise until double again. Put in greased loaf pans and let rise till double in bulk. Bake in a hot oven 10 minutes and a moderate 50 more.

This is good hot or cold. It has a peculiar yellow color from the saffron and a good flavor from the fruit. The use of saffron in English cooking is a very old practice. Since it is a stimulant, it was thought to aid digestion.

Makes 4 loaves.

SPICE SAFFRON BREAD

Add to the above recipe after the first rising:

3 beaten eggs	1 T cinnamon
1 c sugar	1 T nutmeg
3 T caraway seeds	1½ t cloves

This is very good with any hot beverage. It toasts well.

Scones

There are as many varieties of English Scones as Scotch. They are much used in the north of England. Since there are so very many, and since scones will be dealt with more thoroughly in the Scotland section, we give only a few recipes with variations.

OVEN SCONES

2 c flour	2 t B.P.
3 T butter	⅔ c milk
2 T sugar	

Rub the butter into the flour with the finger tips. Add the rest of the ingredients in order, making the whole into a stiff dough. Be careful to handle as little as possible or the scones will be tough. Roll or pat to ½-inch thickness. Cut into rounds, brush with milk, and bake on a greased baking sheet in a hot oven about 10 minutes. "These are quite firm when sufficiently cooked," according to the source of the recipe.

Serve them at once with plenty of butter to make up for the fact that they are not rich in themselves. Excellent for tea or with a salad luncheon. This recipe, in use for years in the Bell family, was brought from Carlisle, England to this country by a relative of the Bell family.

Currant scones.—Add ⅔ c currants; use buttermilk in place of the sweet milk, and ½ t soda in place of the B.P.

Cream scones.—Substitute rich cream for the milk.

Wheaten-meal scones.—Substitute 1 c whole-wheat flour for 1 c white called for. Use sour milk and ½ t soda in place of the sweet milk and B.P.

Makes 1 dozen.

Mrs. Gertrude Martin Tuttle, Bloomfield, New Jersey

FRUIT SCONES

¼ c butter	2 t B.P.
¼ c sugar	½ t salt
1 beaten egg	½ c chopped raisins dates,
½ c milk	currants, or any kind of
3 c flour	dried fruit or candied peel

Cream the butter and sugar. Add the egg and milk. Add the fruit to the sifted-together, dry ingredients. Combine mixtures. Pat out 1-inch thick. Cut in triangles and bake in a hot oven on a greased pan 10-12 minutes.

This is an old-time recipe brought to this country by a woman now nearly 90 years old, a friend of Mrs. Hanson.

Oatmeal scones.—Substitute 1 c ground, rolled oats or steel-cut oatmeal for 1 c of the flour. Omit the fruit.

Whole-meal scones.—Substitute 1½ c of whole-wheat flour for 1½ c of the flour called for. Add 1 t cinnamon. This may be made in one large, round, flat cake and cut in pie-shaped pieces to serve.

Makes about 1½ dozen.

Mrs. H. Hanson, Kirkwood, Missouri

TEA BUNS

All over England there are many, many kinds of tea buns, differing very little in the basic recipe but depending for their flavors and different names on some extra ingredient. For this reason we give a basic tea-bun recipe with variations. Tea buns are often served for breakfast, too.

CURRANT BUN

2 c milk	1 t sugar
¼ c shortening	¼ c milk
½ c sugar	8 c flour
1 t salt	2 c currants
1 beaten egg	½ c chopped peel
1 cake yeast	

Scald the milk, add the shortening, sugar, and salt, and cool. Add the beaten egg and the yeast mixed with the sugar and

¼ c milk. Add the rest in order. Knead well. Let rise till double in bulk. Punch down and shape into flat buns. Let rise (not touching) on a greased baking sheet till double in bulk. Bake 20 minutes in a hot oven.

These buns should be rough on top; the fruit should be covered with dough so it will not burn, but

CURRANT BUNS

the surface should never be smoothed, and only a simple glaze of plain milk or melted butter should be used.

Miss Brown remembers that her Grandmother Chapman from Kent, England, made these often for a very appreciative little girl.

Huffkins.—Omit the fruit and peel. Make large, flat cakes with a hole in the middle. Good for breakfast.

Chudleighs.—Like Huffkins, only smaller.

Morgan tea buns.—Substitute for the currants and peel 2 c chopped almonds.

Rasped rolls.—Grate off the crust of the Yorkshire, or any plain bun, and brown the rest in the oven.

Whigs, also spelled **wiggs,** and said to have been Wordsworth's favorite while at school.—Omit the currants and add 1 t each nutmeg, mace, cloves, and caraway seed. Make it in 6-inch, round, flat cakes that can easily be divided in 4.

Yorkshire buns.—Omit the sugar and add 1 more beaten egg. These are excellent for dinner because they are not sweet.

Yorkshire spiced buns.—Add ½ c raisins, 2 T treacle (molasses), 1 t each cinnamon, cloves, nutmeg, and mace. Mold in oval shapes. Yorkshire is famous for its good cooks. These buns are a good sample.

Makes about 3 dozen buns.

Margaret Jean Brown, Cleveland, Ohio

YORKSHIRE PUDDING

½ c flour	1 egg
⅓ t salt	1 c milk

Break the egg into the salt and flour. Mix gradually. Add half the milk slowly, and beat 10 minutes. The lightness of the pudding depends on this beating. Add the rest of the milk and let stand ½ hour. Cover a pan with the drippings from the roast beef, and heat to boiling. Beat the batter again and pour it over the drippings. Bake in a hot oven 30 minutes, basting it, if liked, with more drippings.

According to Mrs. Hanson, this should be baked before an open fire. If it is baked in the oven it should be called batter pudding. Serve it hot with roast beef and gravy for a special Sunday-dinner treat.

Makes 4 servings.

Mrs. H. Hanson, Kirkwood, Missouri

FRANCE

When one thinks of France and bread, his mouth waters for a generous taste of those long, long loaves of crusty French bread that only the French know how to make really well and that seem never to be affected in flavor or character by the peculiar circumstances under which they are transported from bakery to home. It is nothing to see little boys dragging the yard-long loaves after them in the streets, or old women poking them down in baskets, or, if baskets are lacking, an umbrella. All unwrapped are these long loaves, with no thought given to sanitary regulations, but don't forget, there's character in every inch. It is almost impossible to make them properly at home, for our modern women have not the patience to knead and knead and knead some more to develop all the gluten in the dough, and that must be done to get the maximum of elasticity, a requirement for the dough that makes French bread. *Pain ordinaire* it is if made with water, (in some parts of France it is made

138

with sea water for the special flavor and mineral content);
pain riche if made with milk. But *ordinaire* or *riche,* you
can't find anything better to make you appreciate the French
proverb, "As good as bread."

Then there's the brioche, a deliciously light, delicately
flavored breakfast roll that may be made in pear shapes, large
or small, or may be in any form for that matter, but is still
one of the best accompaniments to morning coffee that was
ever invented by any worthy member of the *Cordon Bleu*
or the *Cordon Rouge.*

Many are the traditions connected with the breads of
France. At Christmastime, in some parts of the country,
the bakers made loaves in the form of circles. With a load
of these on their arms, they go to church, where the bread is
blessed before it becomes a wonderful part of a feast of
special oysters and sausages.

Pancakes, really the first form of bread, have been dressed
up in France until they resemble a paper-thin omelet.
Tradition says that they must be served at New Years, if
good, and riches are to be enjoyed throughout the year; at
Candelmas to insure light bread dough; at Shrovetide to
prevent the grain from decaying.

In France most of the baking is not done in the home
but in the excellent bakeries. However, if we can't run over
to those bakeries, we can at least have a day of fun in the
kitchen and try our hands at a bit of brioche. A good
product we can turn out too, and we'll be tempted to go
French as someone has said and "Eat a meal of bread with
our meal."

APPLE BREAD

2 c warm, thick, un- sweetened applesauce	1 t salt
1 cake yeast	½ c sugar
1 T lard	4 c flour

Add all to the applesauce, mixing well after each addition. Let rise till double in bulk. Punch down. Shape in long loaves; make 3 deep gashes across the top of each and let rise till double in bulk. Bake, touching each other, on a greased baking pan in a hot oven 10 minutes and a moderate 50 more. 10 minutes before it is done, remove from oven, brush with egg white, sprinkle with poppy seed, and return to the oven.

Apple bread is supposed to have been the invention of a Frenchman who said that for their health's sake people should never eat any other kind. It has a good flavor, but not one that can be distinguished as apple. This dough is good made into cinnamon rolls, with lots of B. sugar, butter, and cinnamon. Makes 2 medium-size loaves.

Mrs. Fernand Pierre Brasseur, Cleveland, Ohio

BABA

1 cake yeast	4 T Madeira or other wine
4 T lukewarm water	½ t salt
4¾ c flour	4 T chopped raisins
3 T C. sugar	4 T currants
4 beaten eggs	½ t mace (optional)
½ c cream	½ c chopped, candied
½ c melted butter	orange peel

Dissolve the yeast in the water and add ¾ c of the flour. Beat and let rise 30 minutes. Combine the other ingredients and mix well. Combine the two mixtures adding the rest of the flour. Let rise 1 hour. Put in a round greased mold and let rise about 20 minutes. Bake in a hot oven 10 minutes and a moderate about 50 more.

This is a rich yeast bread, almost cakelike. With a fancy rum sauce, it is often served for dessert. As bread, use it only for breakfast, a salad luncheon, or tea.

Makes 1 loaf.

Mrs. Fernand Pierre Brasseur, Cleveland, Ohio

BRIOCHE

1 cake yeast	½ c sugar
¼ c lukewarm water	1 t salt
1 T sugar	1 beaten egg or 2 yolks
1 c milk	4-5 c flour
3 T butter	1 grated lemon rind

Mix the yeast, water, and 1 T of sugar. Let stand. Scald the milk and add the butter, sugar, and salt. Cool. Add the yeast to the milk mixture. Add the rest of the ingredients, mixing well and using more flour if necessary in kneading the dough. Let rise ½ hour. Knead and shape into buns. Glaze with beaten egg yolk and water and let rise till double. Bake in a hot oven about 20 minutes.

BRIOCHE

There is endless argument as to just what brioche is and how it should be made. Some insist that small, pear-shaped buns with an indentation in the top and a smaller pear shape inserted therein is the real brioche. Some say this pear shape is necessary only when the brioche is made in a large loaf. Some make the buns in crescent shapes, and some are content with a plain round or oval bun. Mme. Brasseur calls hers "couques" and uses this dough as the basis of cinnamon rolls, coffee cake, doughnuts, or tarts. An especially good "couque" is made by lining a muffin tin with this dough, putting a fresh peach in the center, filling the hole with B. sugar, letting it rise 1 hour, and baking it about 30 minutes. Whatever may be your version of brioche or couque, here is a good basic dough for you to do with as you please.

Makes about 2 dozen.

Mme. Alcide Brasseur, Lancaster, Ohio

CROISSANTS (Breakfast Rolls)

¼ c melted butter	1½ t salt
3 stiffly beaten egg whites	¾ c milk
1 cake yeast	4½ c flour
1 T warm water	

Add the eggs to the butter. Soften the yeast in the water and add. Add the rest in order. Mix well. Let rise till double in bulk. Punch down. Shape into croissants by rolling the dough thin, cutting pie-shaped pieces, and rolling these from the large to the small end. These rolls should be about 6 inches long. Glaze with slightly beaten egg white and let rise till double in bulk. Bake in a hot oven about 20 minutes. Glaze again with egg white as they come from the oven.

Nothing is better with morning coffee or chocolate than this unsweetened roll and a sweet brioche for contrast.

Makes about 2 dozen.

Mrs. Fernand Pierre Brasseur, Cleveland, Ohio

CRULLERS

¼ c sugar	1 c flour
½ t salt	3 eggs
¼ c shortening	1 t vanilla or other flavor
1 c boiling water	

Bring the first 4 ingredients to a rapid boil. Add the flour all at once. Mix and cook until it is thick, stirring constantly. When it is slightly cool, add the eggs one at a time, beating well after each addition. Add flavor. Put on greased paper with a pastry tube, making any shape you like. Carefully turn the paper upside down so the crullers will drop into hot fat. Cook until golden brown. Dust with sugar.

These are best eaten warm.

Makes 12-18.

Mrs. Irene Pacot Legros, Mount Vernon, Ohio

PAIN ORDINAIRE (Crusty Bread)

1 cake yeast
¼ c boiled water, cooled
¾ c flour

2 c boiled water, cooled
1½ t salt
6 c flour

Knead the first 3 ingredients into a ball. Make 2 cuts across the top ¼-inch deep. Set the ball in a bowl containing the 2 c water. When the ball floats, add the salt and the rest of the flour. Using more flour if necessary, knead 15 minutes. Let rise till double in bulk. Punch down. Knead again. Shape into long loaves, pointed at the end. Cut a deep furrow in the center of each loaf. Put the loaves, not touching, on a greased baking pan. Let rise till double in bulk. Bake 10 minutes in a hot oven and 50 more in a moderate.

PAIN ORDINAIRE

Brush with beaten egg white and return to the oven about 2 minutes to form a glaze.

This is the delicious French Bread everyone talks about.

Makes 2 medium loaves.

Mmme. Martha Loriaux Pacot, Mount Vernon, Ohio

DOUGHNUTS

½ c shortening
1½ c sugar
4 beaten eggs
1 T lemon juice or brandy

6 c flour
½ t soda
1 t cream of tartar
1 c milk

Cream the shortening and sugar. Add the eggs and lemon juice. Add the sifted-together, dry ingredients alternately with the milk. Mix to a soft dough. Chill ½ hour. Roll thin. Cut in rounds. Make several gashes across the top of each. Fry in hot fat; dust with C. sugar. Use the brandy, if possible, for it gives these a wonderful flavor.

Makes about 4 dozen.

Jennie Frere Delgouffre, Mount Vernon, Ohio

PAIN D'EPICE (Bread of Spices)

2 T lard
½ c B. sugar
1 egg
½ c strong, black coffee
½ c dark corn syrup
1 t cinnamon

1 t soda
3½ c flour
½ t salt
1 c chopped fruit (any dried fruit, peel, or nuts, or any combination of them)

Cream the sugar and lard. Add the egg, and beat well. Add the coffee and syrup and the sifted-together, dry ingredients to which the fruit has been added. Blend. Put in a greased loaf pan and bake in a moderately slow oven about 1 hour.

Cool, slice very thin, and put pieces together with raspberry jam. This is the French way of bringing out the flavor.

Makes 2 medium loaves.

Mme. Alcide Brasseur, Lancaster, Ohio

PAIN RICHE (Potato Bread)

2 medium-sized potatoes
3 c water
1 cake yeast

1 T melted shortening
2 T sugar
2 t salt
7-8 c flour

Cook the potatoes in the water until very soft. Put through a sieve. There should be 2 c of this potato pulp and water. Cool. Add the crumbled yeast, and the rest of the ingredients in order. Knead. Let rise 3 hours. Knead again. Let rise 1 hour more. Knead again and form into long, pointed loaves, using corn meal for rolling dough in while shaping the loaf. Gash the top with 3 diagonal gashes. Glaze with beaten egg white. Let rise on a greased pan, the loaves not touching, until double in bulk. Bake in a hot oven 10 minutes and a moderate about 50 more. For a soft crust, put a small pan of water in the oven to steam while the bread is baking. Most people like the harder crust.

Makes 2 medium loaves.

Mme. Jennie Frere Delgouffre, Mount Vernon, Ohio

SAVARIN

Use the recipe for brioche (p. 141) making it in round loaves. Stick it all over with slices of candied peel, cherries, and almonds, and brush it with slightly beaten egg white. Sprinkle thickly with sugar. Let rise till double in bulk and bake in a hot oven 10 minutes and a moderate 40 more.

Makes 2 medium loaves.

Mme. Alcide Brasseur, Lancaster, Ohio

GERMANY

Germany and its kuchen!—Apple, cherry, prune, nut, crumb. The German housewife knows every conceivable way to dress up a good piece of yeast dough to make it a perfect delight, especially with afternoon coffee, if you follow the old country custom, or for Sunday breakfast if you are afraid of the pounds connected with the afternoon coffee.

It's quite a step from the rich kuchen made with white flour, the mark of the upper classes in Germany, to the dark rye of the lower classes. But people make that step without difficulty. The pumpernickel is so good in its own sour, dour way, especially with a bit of well-flavored wurst or some really powerful cheese, that it makes its own friends regardless of class distinctions. If one feels the real thing is a bit too sour and heavy, if he can't quite like the aromatic flavor, then let him be content with the lighter variety we ordinarily have in this country.

For a delicate but healthful accompaniment to morning coffee or chocolate, there's nothing like a good old German zwieback. It's nothing but a good bread dough twice baked, but in that extra baking there is a world of flavor. Real German chocolate is apt to be a bit too rich for ordinary consumption; the zwieback balances that tendency perfectly with its airy crumbiness. The world owes Hamburg a debt of culinary gratitude, for it is said that zwieback was invented there.

You'll need plenty of the "makings of things" for these German breads, but you'll be glad you had the opportunity to blend them into a perfect product.

FASNACHT KUECHLE (Fast Night Cakes)

1 c mashed, unsalted potatoes	2 T butter
1 c potato water	¾ c sugar
1 cake yeast	1 beaten egg
½ c water	1 t salt
2 c flour	½ c lukewarm water
	5 c flour

Mix the first 5 ingredients and let stand overnight. In the morning add the next 4, creamed together. Add the water and flour. Beat well. Let rise till double in bulk. Punch down. Roll ¼-inch thick. Cut in squares. Let rise ½ hour. Drop the squares in hot fat to fry like doughnuts.

This may be used as doughnuts or coffee-cake dough, decorated, and baked in a moderate oven 40-60 minutes. It's a good idea to use half this way and half in the kuechle.

This is a real old German recipe that has been served in the Bentz family for years and years and years as a necessary accompaniment to a bean-soup dinner.

Other tradition says that these must be eaten Shrove Tuesday, the day before Lent begins.

Makes about 6 dozen.

Mrs. E. V. Bentz, Chillicothe, Ohio

FASNACHT KUECHLE (Fancy)

1 beaten egg   1 c flour
¼ t salt   1 t B.P.
½ c milk

FASNACHT KUECHLE

Mix in order and beat well. Have lard hot for frying as for dougnuts. Hold your finger over the small end of a funnel until you have 6 T of the batter in the large end. Then let the batter drip slowly into the hot fat as you move the funnel around in circles. When this spiral kuechle is brown on one side, turn and brown it on the other. Drain and refill the funnel for a second kuechle.

According to Mrs. Bentz, "This is a real old German recipe and a favorite in our family. They should be served while hot and are real nice with a bean-soup dinner." These are not as difficult to make as it seems.

Makes about 4.

Mrs. E. V. Bentz, Chillicothe, Ohio

FASNACHT KUECHLE (Quick)

3 beaten eggs   ⅔ t salt
2 c milk   8-9 c flour
1 T softened butter

Mix in order given. Roll out ¼-inch thick. Cut in squares. Fry in hot fat like doughtnuts.

These are not sweet and make a good soup or salad accompaniment. They are better served hot.

Makes about 6 dozen.

Mrs. E. V. Bentz, Chillicothe, Ohio

GINGERBREAD

6 egg yolks	3 c flour
2 c sugar	¼ c finely cut citron
1 c corn syrup	1 c chopped nuts
3 t B.P.	1 c milk
1 t cinnamon	¼ c grated bitter chocolate
¼ t ginger	(melted)
½ t soda	3 stiffly beaten egg whites

Beat the egg yolks well. Add the sugar, and beat 2 minutes. Stir in the syrup. Add the fruit and nuts to the sifted-together, dry ingredients. Add this mixture to the first, alternately with the milk. Stir in the chocolate, and fold in the egg whites. Bake in greased loaf pans in a moderate oven 1 hour. Cool.

This is a rich gingerbread, with a different flavor because of the chocolate.

It is good with afternoon coffee.

Makes 2 medium loaves.

HUTZEL BREAD (Spiced Pear)

2 c spiced pear juice	1 t fennel seed
¼ c butter	2 t cinnamon
½ c lard	2 beaten eggs
1 t salt	1 cake yeast
1 c B. sugar	⅓ c lukewarm water
2 c raisins	1 T sugar
3 c chopped, spiced pears	12 c flour

Scald the pear juice. Add the next 8 ingredients. Cool. Add the eggs and the yeast mixed with the water and sugar. Add the flour and mix well. Let rise overnight. In the morning punch down and put in greased loaf pans, using a spoon, as the dough is too sticky to handle. Let rise till double in bulk and bake in a hot oven 10 minutes and a moderate 50 more.

This fruitcakelike bread keeps well about a week. It is fine flavored whether hot or cold. The use of spiced pears is a tradition in German baking.

Makes 4 loaves.

KUCHEN

There are so many, many kinds of kuchen, that cakelike bread, that a whole book could be written about them alone. We give two kuchen recipes: The first is a very good, plain kuchen; the second is richer in every respect. Take your choice of these and use them as the basis of the variations suggested.

PLAIN KUCHEN

1 c boiling water	2 c cold water
2 t salt	1 cake yeast
1 c sugar	2 beaten eggs
2 T butter	12 c flour
2 T lard	

Pour the boiling water over the next 4 ingredients. Add the cold water. Crumble the yeast in. Add the eggs and the flour a little at a time, working it carefully as you add. This may now be put in the refrigerator and used as desired or used at once. If used now let rise 1 hour. Knead down. Shape into any kind of kuchen desired. Let rise till double in bulk. Bake in a moderate oven about 30 minutes or more, depending on the size of the kuchen.

Mrs. Kistemaker, who has made these kuchen every Saturday night, "since goodness knows when," and, "for a big family too, mind you—there's never any left for Sunday," has some good advice to offer in the handling of yeast. "Never, never put the yeast in the boiling water. Just remember that what your hand can stand, the yeast can stand, and remember that yeast don't like a draft, and remember when you knead the dough, don't be afraid to hurt it; just slap it around and stretch it and slap it some more."

Makes 4 kuchen.

Mrs. John Kistemaker, Cleveland, Ohio

RICH KUCHEN

1 c milk	2 beaten eggs
1 c shortening	1 beaten egg yolk
½ c sugar	½ t salt
1 cake yeast	1 t cinnamon
2 T lukewarm water	5 c flour

Scald the milk and add the shortening and sugar. Cool. Add the yeast mixed with the water. Add the rest in order given. Mix well. Let rise till double in bulk. Punch down and let rise again. Flatten out on a greased pan. Brush with slightly beaten egg white. Sprinkle with sugar and cinnamon. Nuts or coconut may be used too. Make depressions at 1-inch intervals so the "goo" will go into the kuchen. Let rise till double in bulk, and bake in a moderate oven about 40 minutes.

VARIATIONS

Make all these variations from the once-risen dough. After shaping them, let them rise till double in bulk and bake in a moderate oven about 40-50 minutes, depending on the size of the kuchen.

APFELKUCHEN

Apfelkuchen (apple).—Flatten the dough out in a greased, shallow pan. Put rows of raw apple slices on top. Sprinkle well with cinnamon and sugar. Dot with butter. Any such fruit as peaches, plums, prunes, grapes (seeded), cherries (seeded), may be used in the same way.

Bund kuchen.—Put in round, bund form. Glaze when cold.

Butter-zopf (twist).—Divide the dough in 3 parts. Make these into 3 ropes. Braid together, making the loaf larger in the middle than at the ends. Brush with butter and sprinkle with sugar. Or glaze when baked.

Käsekuchen (cheese).—Line a shallow pan with dough and fill with this filling:

1 c cottage cheese	4 beaten eggs
6 T melted butter	1 c currants
¼ c sugar	¼ c chopped almonds
¼ t salt	

Mix all together.

Kugel.—Add 1 c raisins, 1 c chopped peel. Put in round, tube pan. Sprinkle with B. sugar and finely chopped almonds. Very good toasted.

Kranz kuchen (filled).—Put a layer of dough in the bottom of a round loaf pan. Cover with filling:

FILLING

1 c chopped almonds	¼ c cream
½ c macaroon or zwieback crumbs	1 c seedless raisins
	1 T sugar

Put another layer of dough on top.

Mincemeat kuchen.—Spread kuchen with mincemeat. Cover with a mixture of 1 beaten egg, ¼ c sour cream, ¼ c sugar.

Mohn kuchen (poppy seed).—Roll out ½-inch-thick sheet of dough. Spread with filling, roll as jelly roll, and bake in a greased loaf pan.

FILLING

1 c ground poppy seeds	½ c chopped raisins
½ t grated lemon rind	¼ t ginger
1 T butter	½ t cinnamon
½ c corn syrup	2 T grated chocolate

Cook all but the chocolate. When it is thick, add it.

Napf kuchen.—Add 1 T grated lemon peel and ⅓ c chopped almonds. Put the dough in a napf or turk's-head pan lined with buttered crumbs.

Streussel kuchen (crumb).—Rub together ½ c sugar, ½ c flour, and ½ c butter, with 1 t vanilla, and ½ c ground almonds.

Sprinkle it over the kuchen, pressing in a bit (this is sometimes called rivels).

Makes about 2 kuchen.

PUMPERNICKEL

¾ c corn meal	1 T caraway seed
1½ c cold water	2 c mashed potatoes
1½ c boiling water	1 cake yeast
1½ T salt	¼ c lukewarm water
2 T sugar	4 c rye flour
2 T shortening	4¼ c white flour

Stir the cold water into the corn meal, add the boiling water, and cook, stirring constantly for 2 minutes. Add salt, sugar, shortening, and caraway, and let stand until lukewarm. Add potatoes and yeast mixed with the water, then the flours. Knead till smooth, using corn meal on the board. Place in a greased bowl. Turn so as to grease all sides. Let rise till double in bulk. Knead again. Put in greased pans. Let rise till double in bulk. Bake in a hot oven 10 minutes and a moderate 50 more.

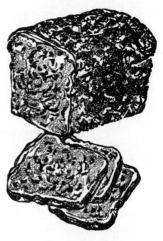

PUMPERNICKEL

This dark, moist bread, so good in cheese sandwiches, will keep well for a week.

Makes 3 loaves.

POTATO PANCAKES

6 medium-sized potatoes grated fine (about 2 c)	1 t salt
2 beaten eggs	2 t B.P.
	½ c flour

Mix and blend. Fry in butter over a low fire. Brown on both sides.

These are a great German delicacy for which the taste should be cultivated. They make a good Saturday night main dish with only fruit and coffee besides.

Makes enough for 6.

Mrs. John Kistemaker, Cleveland, Ohio

RYE BLACK BREAD

2 cakes yeast	2 T salt
1 T water	10 c rye flour
1 t sugar	8 c white flour
4½ c water	1 T caraway (optional)

Mix the first 3. Add the rest in order and knead well. Let rise till double in bulk. Knead again and shape into loaves. Let rise on greased pans till it is double in bulk. Bake in a hot oven 10 minutes and a moderate 60 more.

This is dark and sour; it is supposed to be.

Makes 4 large loaves.

SEMIKUCHEN (Quick)

1 beaten egg	4 t B.P.
¾ c milk	½ t salt
½ c sugar	3 T melted shortening
2 c flour	

Add the milk and sugar to the egg. Add the sifted-together, dry ingredients and the melted butter. Mix well. Put in a greased shallow pan. Sprinkle with sugar and cinnamon and dot with butter. Bake in a hot oven 20 minutes.

Semikuchen means that this is not a yeast kuchen, but like one. It is quickly made and very good. Some call it Blitz Kuchen.

Makes 1 kuchen.

Mrs. E. V. Bentz, Chillicothe, Ohio

SCHENECKEN (Sweet Snails)

½ c milk	1 cake yeast
½ c shortening	½ c sugar
2 beaten eggs	1½ t salt
1 c sour cream	5 c flour

Scald the milk and add the shortening. Cool. Add the eggs and sour cream. Crumble the yeast in the sugar and let stand till it liquifies. Add to the first mixture. Add the salt and flour. Beat well—the longer the better. Place in refrigerator overnight. Next morning, let the dough rise to double in bulk. Punch down and add 1 more c flour. Knead well. Roll out in thin sheets. Cover them with sugar, cinnamon, chopped nuts, and raisins, sprinkled thickly. Roll as jelly roll. Cut in ½-inch pieces and place on a greased baking sheet or put in greased muffin pans. Let rise till double in bulk. Bake in a moderately hot oven about 30 minutes.

SCHENECKEN

These are delicious for breakfast. Little "sweet snails" they are in name and looks. They may be frosted with C. sugar and water mixed to spread.

Makes about 2 dozen.

Mrs. Mary Lintner Lewis, Rio Grande, Ohio

SOUR-CREAM TWISTS

Use the same dough as for schenecken, omitting the sugar and softening the yeast in ¼ c water. Remove the dough from the refrigerator. Roll out in a sheet. Sprinkle it with sugar. Fold the sides and ends together so that all the sugar is covered. Roll again. Repeat this until you have used 1 c sugar. Cut oblong strips of dough. Shape into twists. Let rise till double in bulk. Bake on an ungreased baking sheet in a hot oven about 20 minutes.

Makes about 3 dozen.

STÖLLEN

2 c milk	⅓ c chopped citron
1 c sugar	½ c currants
2 t salt	½ c assorted candied fruit
1⅓ c shortening	(cherries, pineapple, etc.)
2 cakes yeast	1 grated lemon rind
8 c flour	2 t vanilla
4 beaten eggs	extra fruit and nuts in
1½ c chopped, blanched	large pieces for decora-
almonds	tion (optional)
1½ c raisins	

Scald the milk. Add the sugar, salt, and shortening. Cool. Crumble in the yeast and add 2 c of the flour. Let rise till light and bubbly. Add the rest of the in-

STÖLLEN

gredients in order. Knead until the dough is smooth and elastic. Divide it in 3 parts. Roll out in ½-inch-thick, oval shapes. Sprinkle with sugar and cinnamon. Fold edges together as for an omelet, making long loaves, narrow at the ends. Brush the tops with melted butter and let rise on a greased pan till double in bulk. Bake in a hot oven 10 minutes and a moderate oven 50 more.

This is the traditional Christmas loaf called Christöllen, Christmas Coffee Cake, or Christmas Bread. It is delicious and will keep well so that it is always on hand for the unexpected holiday guest. It is often served for Christmas breakfast, after-noon coffee, or with wine in place of fruitcake. There is not a nicer Christmas gift than a stöllen frosted with C. sugar-and-water icing and decorated with large pieces of fruit and nuts in traditional Christmas designs. With a cellophane wrapper and a gay ribbon, you have a beautiful loaf.

Makes 2 stöllen.

Mrs. Sylvia Kuechle, Cleveland, Ohio

STUFFED BREAD

FILLING

2½ c chopped, dried fruit
(figs, dates, raisins,
prunes, pears, currants,
etc.)
½ c chopped candied peel

¾ c chopped nuts
½ t cinnamon
⅛ lb. melted sweet chocolate

DOUGH

1 cake yeast
1 t water
½ t sugar
2 T milk
1 T sugar

1 t salt
2 beaten eggs
½ c melted shortening
3 c flour

Mix the first 3 ingredients. Add the rest in order and mix well. Let rise 1 hour. Take 1 c of bread dough and mix it with the filling, working it well until the whole mass is incorporated. Shape into a narrow loaf. Roll out the rest of the dough ½-inch thick. Put the fruit loaf inside and cover it completely with the sheet of dough. Moisten and pinch the edges together. Brush with slightly beaten egg. Let rise 1 hour. Bake in a slow oven about 1 hour.

This is really a loaf within a loaf. When the bread is cut, there will be the fruit loaf encircled with the bread dough. Very attractive it is, good for luncheon, afternoon coffee, or with a beverage in the evening.

Makes 1 large loaf.

ZWIEBACK

½ c milk, scalded and
cooled
2 cakes yeast
½ t salt
¼ c sugar

¼ c melted shortening
3 beaten eggs
4–5 c flour

Add the crumbled yeast to the milk. Add the salt and 1 c of the flour. Let rise till bubbly. Add the rest of the ingredients in order. Mix well. Let rise till double in bulk. Punch down and knead well. Put in a greased loaf pan and let rise till double in bulk. Bake in a hot oven 10 minutes and a moderate about 35 more. When cold, slice in 1-inch-thick pieces, return to the oven, and brown on both sides slowly until crisp throughout. These will keep well and are delicious for breakfast. Mighty good for children, too.

Makes 2 loaves.

ZWIEBEL KUCHEN (Onion)

2 c sliced dry onions	1/4 c sugar
3 T butter	1 c sour cream
1 t salt	1 T flour
3 beaten eggs	

Cook the sliced onions slowly in the butter about 20 minutes. Cool. Add the remaining ingredients in order and mix. Line a pie pan with any bread or kuchen dough, and pour the onion mixture on top. Bake in a moderate oven about 45 minutes. Serve hot or cold with salad luncheon, or as a snack.

Makes 1 kuchen.

ZEKE'S BLITZ KUCHEN

1 c sugar	1 1/2 c flour
1/4 c shortening	1 t B.P.
2 beaten egg yolks	1/2 t salt
1/2 c milk	2 stiffly beaten egg whites
1/2 t vanilla	

Cream the sugar and shortening. Add the egg yolks, milk, and vanilla. Add the sifted-together dry ingredients. Fold in the stiffly beaten egg whites. Pour in a greased loaf pan. Sprinkle with sugar, cinnamon, and finely cut almonds, or brown sugar, butter, and any kind of nuts. Bake in a moderate oven about 30 minutes.

Mrs. Haven L. Zebold, Cleveland, Ohio

HEBREW

The Hebrew people have been condemned to a life of wandering, and, unfortunate as this may have been in some respects, it has proved to be a great boon to their cooking. They have borrowed the culinary secrets of every people with whom they have been long in contact. To these borrowings they have added their own deft touch with the result that good Hebrew baking is for the gourmet.

The matzoth, Passover bread of Biblical times, originally made in rounds or squares four inches thick, is the Hebrews own contribution to the bread family. It is made of flour and water only, and baked until dry. Originally it was dried in the sun. In these days it is made commercially, sold in packaged form, and used the year round as bread, crackers, toast, or, when ground fine, in such things as griddlecakes, piecrust, or muffins, as a part of the flour. People who are not used to the flat taste have to cultivate a liking for matzoth, which they can do quite easily by using it as a basis for snappy cheese or highly flavored meat spreads.

On the Hebrew bread plate, you will find kugelhupf that will remind you of Austria; coffee cakes that surely were brought from Germany; pancakes that might have come from France; light rye bread like that of Czechoslovakia; and the very dark rye that suggests Russia. Hebrew baking, then, may best be described by the word eclectic.

BUTTER BRAIDS

1 cake yeast	2 c milk, scalded and
½ c lukewarm water	cooled
1 t salt	1 grated lemon rind
1 T sugar	¼ c raisins
¼ c butter	2 well-beaten eggs
½ c sugar	9 c flour

Mix the first 4 ingredients and let stand ½ hour. Cream the butter and sugar and add to the first. Add the rest in order.

Let rise till double in bulk. Punch down. Knead. Divide the dough into 6 ropes and braid, making 2 braids, 1 smaller than the other. Put the smaller on top of the larger, tapering both at the ends. Brush with beaten egg, sprinkle with poppy seeds, let rise till double in bulk, and bake on a greased pan in a hot oven 10 minutes and a moderate 40 more.

BUTTER BRAID

If these are to be served at a meat meal, use water in place of milk and vegetable shortening instead of butter.

Makes 2 braids.

KRAPFEN (Doughnuts)

Use the butter braid dough, increasing the butter to ½ c, the sugar to 1 c, and omitting the raisins. Roll as thin as paper.

Cut in rounds. Spread the edges with beaten egg to keep the filling from running. Spread with 1 t jelly, jam, or marmalade. Put a top on and pinch the edges together. Spread with melted butter. Let rise 1 hour. Fry as doughnuts, putting the side that was down while rising up first while frying. Dust with C. sugar.

These will have white stripes around the middle.

Makes about 4 dozen.

Donna Gitlin, Columbus, Ohio

KICHLECH (Egg Crackers)

2 beaten eggs

1¼ c flour

½ t salt

½ t B.P.

Mix to a dough, and knead on a floured board till firm. Roll thin and cut in large diamonds. Sprinkle with sugar. Prick all over with a fork. Bake on a floured, but not greased, baking sheet in a moderately hot oven 15-20 minutes.

KICHLECH

These are good with salads or cold drinks. They should be eaten while fresh.

Makes about 1 dozen.

Donna Gitlin, Columbus, Ohio

KUCHEN

The kuchen are so much like the German variety (pp. 150-151) that it is unnecessary to include the recipe. Use the German with all the variations suggested and these in addition:

Breakfast roll.—Roll out a ½-inch-thick sheet of dough. Cut triangles and put 2 together with chopped almonds, raisins, and citron. Pinch edges to hold filling. Lay in greased pan two inches apart. Spread with beaten egg white and a few chopped almonds. Let rise until double in bulk and bake in a hot oven about 20 minutes.

Filled coffee cake.—Roll ½-inch-thick sheet of dough. Sprinkle with sugar and dots of butter. Fold dough over and roll flat. Repeat twice. Then sprinkle with chopped walnuts. Fold over and roll ½-inch-thick. Put in greased shallow pan, dot with butter, and sprinkle with more walnuts, cinnamon, and sugar. Let rise till double in bulk and bake in a moderate oven 30-40 minutes. Cut in squares and serve.

Mohn cakes (poppy seed).—Roll sheet of dough ½-inch-thick. Cut in strips. Sprinkle with poppy seeds that have been soaked in water ½ hour and drained. Let rise till double, and bake in a hot oven about 20 minutes. Use poppy seeds generously in any Hebrew baking—for sprinkling and in addition to or in place of any filling used.

Parsley platz.—Same as zweibel under Germany (p. 158), using parsley in place of onions.

Roly poly.—Roll thin sheet of dough. Brush with butter and sprinkle with chopped almonds, chopped raisins, and currants. Fold over 3 inches of the dough. Sprinkle this part. Fold 3 inches and sprinkle again. Repeat till all the dough is used and it looks like a flat roly poly. Brush with egg, let rise till double in bulk, and bake in a moderate oven about 1 hour.

Spice roll.—Roll dough ½-inch-thick. Sprinkle with grated lebkuchen or gingerbread, chopped almonds, raisins, currants, B. sugar, spice, and dots of butter. Roll as for jelly roll. Let rise on a greased pan till double in bulk. Bake in a hot oven 10 minutes and in a moderate about 30 more.

KUGELHUPF

1 cake yeast	½ t salt
1 T lukewarm water	1 c milk, scalded and
1 c shortening	cooled
1 T sugar	½ c chopped raisins
1 c C. sugar	½ c chopped citron
4 beaten egg yolks	5 c flour
1 grated lemon rind	3 stiffly beaten egg whites

Mix the first 3 and let stand 5 minutes. Cream the sugar and shortening. Add to the yeast. Add the rest in order, beating hard five minutes before folding in the egg whites. Pour in a well-greased tube pan and let rise till double in bulk. Bake in a moderate oven 45-50 minutes.

This is a rich, flavorful, cakelike bread, fine with afternoon coffee.

Makes 2 loaves.

Donna Gitlin, Columbus, Ohio

MANDEL BREAD (Almond)

3 eggs	1½ c flour
½ c sugar	½ c finely chopped, blanched
2 t B.P.	almonds

Beat the eggs and sugar until very thick. Add the sifted-together, dry ingredients and almonds. Mix carefully. Put into a well-greased long loaf pan and bake 45 minutes in a moderate oven.

Makes 1 loaf.

Donna Gitlin, Columbus, Ohio

MATZO GRIDDLECAKES

3 matzo leaves	½ t cinnamon
1½ c hot water	1 T sugar
3 beaten eggs	½ t salt
1 T melted chicken fat, goose grease, or butter	

Soak the matzos in the hot water. Drain, and to the soaked matzos add the rest in order. Bake as pancakes and serve with jelly, or any sweet filling.

These are not like our griddlecakes and should not be compared to them.

Makes about 6.

SOUP CAKES

2 beaten eggs   1½ c flour
2 T melted chicken fat   ¾ c water
1 t B.P.

Mix all till smooth. Pour greased muffin pans ⅔ full and bake in a moderate oven about 45 minutes.

These are odd in looks and flavor, but good. They rise only at the sides and form a hollow in the center of each cake. Serve with soup or salad.

Makes 1 dozen.

Donna Gitlin, Columbus, Ohio

TURNOVERS

1 c heavy, sour cream   2 t salt
2 beaten eggs   3 c flour
½ c melted butter   2 t B.P.

Mix in order given. Roll dough ¼-inch thick. Cut in 4-inch squares. Put a spoonful of filling on each. Fold edges together to form triangles. Moisten and pinch well to hold the filling. Prick the tops once. Bake on a greased baking sheet in a moderate oven 30-45 minutes.

FILLING

1 c cottage cheese   1 beaten egg
1 c grated yellow cheese   1 t salt
¼ c melted butter

Mix all well.

These turnovers should be used soon after baking. They are fine with salad, beverages, and soups.

Makes 2 dozen.

Donna Gitlin, Columbus, Ohio

ZWIEBACK

Omit the almonds in Mandel Bread and add 1 t anise flavoring. When it is cold, cut in 1-inch slices and return to the oven to dry out.

Makes about 1 dozen.

Donna Gitlin, Columbus, Ohio

HOLLAND

The people of Holland, with their love of good, rich, and substantial foods, have some wonderful breads to put in the international breadbasket. Here again we find the ever-popular kuchen with all its variations, the spicy honeycake, the breads for special days, Easter and Christmas, with a world of tradition behind them. The traditions are so closely connected with individual recipes given here that we have included them with the recipes rather than in this introduction.

DRIEKONINGENBROOD (Kings' Bread)

Use the recipe for sugar cake (p. 170), adding 2 more eggs and 2 almonds. Here is Mrs. Constandse's description:

"Any white bread recipe may be used with addition of one or more eggs. It has the form and about the size as a round rye bread. Only once a year in honor of the Three Wise Kings of the Orient, this bread is enjoyed. In it is baked one almond and the person re-

ceiving the slice with the almond, whether whole or the
largest part of it, is considered the wisest person and
must then proceed to produce another Driekoningen-
brood. Often to the great hilarity of the family or
others present. As a rule, this bread is ordered from
the baker instead of baked at home."

Makes 2 loaves.

Mrs. Clara Constandse, Cleveland, Ohio

GINGERBREAD

½ c melted butter	¼ c chopped, candied orange
4 c dark corn syrup	peel
¼ t coriander seed	2 beaten eggs
2 T caraway seed	16 c flour
4 T ginger	

Mix in order, to a stiff dough. Put in greased loaf pans and
bake in a moderately hot oven 45 minutes.

This is solid, but full of good flavors. It is a very old recipe,
hence the large amounts. Cut to ¼ for ordinary family.

Makes 8 loaves.

KOESISTERS (Old Dutch Sweet Meat)

3 c flour	½ t salt
1 c B. sugar	1 t mixed spice
½ c butter	4 beaten eggs
2 t cinnamon	1 cake yeast
	1 T warm water

Mix the flour and sugar. Cut in the butter. Add the rest in
order, the yeast having been softened in the water. Let rise till
double in bulk. Knead. Roll ¾-inch thick. Cut in 2-inch
squares and fry in hot fat till brown on both sides. Cool.
Dip in syrup made of 3 c sugar, 1 t cinnamon, and 2 c water,
boiled 4 minutes and cooled. Dry them out before serving.

These are unusual and good; will keep for months.

Makes about 2 dozen.

KRENTENBROOD (Currant Bread)

1½ cakes yeast	1 T melted shortening
1½ t sugar	2 t salt
¾ c lukewarm milk	4 T chopped citron
3¾ c flour	½ c currants
1 beaten egg	½ c raisins

Dissolve the yeast and sugar in ¼ c of the milk. Add the rest of the milk, the egg, and half the flour. Mix well. Let rise till double in bulk. Add the rest of the ingredients, beating well after each addition. Knead until smooth and elastic. Let rise till double in bulk, about 2 hours. Put in greased loaf pan and let rise till double in bulk. Bake in a hot oven 10 minutes and a moderate 40 more.

"Krentenbrood is also called 'Paaschbrood' or Easter-bread! In fact it is called just that around Eastertime. A very interesting custom prevailed in The Netherlands which since the outbreak of the World War ceased to be. Every baker would give to his regular customers a Paaschbrood; the better the customer, the more Paaschbrooden that family or person would receive. This brood was always light (well risen), had a brown shining crust, and was just loaded with currants, citron, and raisins, the latter two being the half of the melange and the currants making the other half. The length of the brood also varied in accordance to customer. They varied in length anywhere from 1½ feet to over 1 yard. Those extremely long ones were rarely found in some provinces. In Groninger they were popular; in Nord-Hollard the bakers preferred to increase the amount rather by the number of loaves for a 'good customer'. The thickness of the bread was rarely more than 5-6 inches, was flat at bottom, and half round on the top.

"To make the Easter joy complete, the milkman would never forget to deliver free of charge a small tin can with sweet cream enough for 5 or 6 cups of coffee; this was delivered on Easter Sunday and the bread usually on Good Friday. Another charming habit gone out of existence during World War I."

Makes 1 large loaf.

Mrs. Clara Constandse, Cleveland, Ohio

MASHED-POTATO KUCHEN OR DOUGHNUTS

½ c mashed potatoes	1 cake yeast
½ c potato water	1 t lukewarm water
½ c shortening	2 beaten eggs
1 t salt	½ c sugar
½ c sugar	1½ c flour
3¾ c flour	

Mix the first 6 ingredients. Add the yeast softened in the water. Mix well. Let stand overnight. In the morning add the remaining ingredients and knead. Put on a greased shallow tin, and brush with melted butter. Sprinkle with "rivels" made of ½ c flour, ¼ c sugar, and 1 T beaten egg yolk rubbed with the hands to form crumbs. Let rise till double in bulk, and bake in a moderate oven 40 minutes.

Add 1 t of your favorite spice and use this for doughnuts. (See p. 62 for frying directions.) Tender and moist.

Makes 2 kuchen or 4 dozen doughnuts.

MOSCOVISCH GEBAK (Pastry)

1¼ c flour	⅛ t salt
½ c butter	4 eggs beaten separately
¾ c raisins and currants, mixed	¾ c sugar
4 T finely chopped citron	

Cut the butter into the flour. Add the fruit, peel, and salt. Beat the egg yolks with the sugar. Add the first mixture to the egg mixture. Fold in the stiffly beaten egg whites. Do not beat or stir, but blend it very lightly. Put it in a buttered tube pan lined with fine zwieback crumbs. Bake in a moderately hot oven 45 minutes.

"This gebak is used with mid-morning coffee or as dessert for luncheon or dinner."

Makes 1 loaf.

Mrs. Clara Constandse, Cleveland, Ohio

ONTBYKOEK (Honey Bread)

2 c unsifted flour
¾ c B. sugar
1 T B.P.
2 t cinnamon
¼ t each cloves and
  nutmeg

1 t soda
¼ t salt
1 c sour milk or buttermilk
¼ c honey (dark corn syrup
  may be used)
1 well-beaten egg

Mix the dry ingredients. Add the liquids and blend well. Bake in well-greased loaf pans in a moderate oven 45-60 minutes.

"This is a very popular bread all over The Netherlands, although slightly different recipes are used, and is known by various names as: Honey Kuchen, Breakfast Kuchen, Cut Kuchen, and a few more. It may be cut like bread and buttered and

ONTBYKOEK

thus eaten, or after slicing it put onto a buttered slice of bread. Children like it very much. This koek belongs to the variety which is used in Friesland (North Eastern Province) to put on a child's arm when it has a birthday. . . ."

For a variation add 2 T chopped almonds, ½ c chopped figs, ½ c each raisins and currants, and let the dough stand in the pan 20 minutes before baking.

Makes 1 large loaf.

Mrs. Clara Constandse, Cleveland, Ohio

SEED BISKET

1 c milk	1 T caraway seeds
¾ c butter	2 cakes yeast
½ c sugar	1 c lukewarm water
1 t salt	1 T sugar
	10 c flour

Scald the milk; add the next 4 ingredients. Cool. Add the yeast that has been mixed with the water and sugar and allowed to stand 1 hour. Add the flour, and mix well. Let rise till double in bulk. Knead. Roll in a thin sheet. Cut biscuit. Let rise on a greased baking sheet till double in bulk. Bake in a hot oven 10-15 minutes.

Makes about 5 dozen.

SUGAR CAKE WITH VARIATIONS

1 c milk	1 beaten egg
⅓ c sugar	1 cake yeast
½ t salt	2 T warm water
¼ c shortening	4 c flour

Scald the milk and add the next 3 ingredients. Cool. Add the egg, the yeast softened in water, and the flour. Knead well. Let rise till double in bulk. Knead again. Put in a large, round, greased baking pan and let rise till double in bulk. Spread with melted butter; sprinkle with sugar, cinnamon, and chopped nuts. Bake in a hot oven 10 minutes and a moderate 50 more.

Dutch apple cake.—Pat the dough into shallow, greased pans. Cover it with thin, raw apple slices, dots of butter, sugar, and cinnamon. Let rise till double and bake in a moderately hot oven about 40 minutes.

Oliebollen (fat rolls).—Add to the risen dough, 1 c currants, ½ c raisins, 2 T chopped peel, and 2 c finely grated sour apples. Let rise again till double in bulk. Drop by spoonfuls in hot fat and fry as doughnuts. Serve at once.

Sticky buns.—Roll dough in sheet. Brush with melted butter. Cover with currants, raisins, cut citron, nuts, B. sugar, and cinnamon in generous amounts. Roll as jelly roll. Cut in 1-inch pieces and stand them close together in a high-sided pan dotted

SUGAR CAKE

with butter and covered with ¼-inch of light corn syrup. Let rise till double. Bake in a moderately hot oven about 30 minutes. Remove from pan at once. Makes 2 loaves or about 3 dozen small forms.

For all other kuchen, schnecken, etc., see German kuchen variations (p. 151).

HUNGARY

Hungarians claim that their flour is the best in the world. They claim, too, that their peasant loaves, weighing as much as twelve pounds each, are the very best. Impossible as it may sound, the peasant is supposed to consume not one but three of these enormous loaves in a week. Naturally, he has little else to eat and naturally, considering how good the flour is and what excellent cooks the Hungarians are, the bread is excellent.

Hungarian baking is marked by great variety because in early days Hungary lay on the trade routes east, and, as the caravans passed back and forth, she borrowed whatever she liked in the way of culinary ideas. What is more important, she seemed to like only the best.

You must be prepared to be what is called a rich cook when you try many of these recipes. You'll find them calling for much sour cream, and it must be rich, many eggs, pounds and pounds of butter, almonds in profusion, and spices of all varieties; but you'll never regret an ingredient no matter how expensive when you taste the coffee cake, the various horns, the doughnuts—that are thought by some to be the best in the world—the fruit bread and the nut tart.

Since Hungarian cookery is eclectic, you'll be finding things that will remind you of some other country, such as the coffee cake of Germany; but be assured that if the Hungarians have chosen to take a coffee cake or any other recipe, they have dressed it up to make it their own, and their own is delicious.

BACON SCRAP BISCUIT

½ c finely chopped, cooked bacon	2 beaten eggs
8 c flour	1 t salt
1¼ c sour cream	1 cake yeast
	¼ c milk

Mix in order, adding the yeast softened in the milk last. Form a dough. Knead. Roll 1-inch thick. Cut. Mark the tops with crosses made with a sharp knife. Let rise on a greased pan till double in bulk. Brush with beaten egg yolk. Bake in a hot oven 15-20 minutes.

These have a wonderful flavor from the combination of bacon and sour cream. Good with salad luncheon.

Makes 6 dozen.

BUTTER BISCUIT

1 c butter	2 t salt
6 c flour	2 c sour cream

Cut the butter into the flour. Add the rest to form a soft dough. Roll ½-inch thick. Cut. Brush with beaten egg yolk, and bake on a greased pan in a hot oven 12-15 minutes.

Makes 4 dozen.

BISCUIT (Puff Paste)

2 c lard	1½ t salt
4 c flour	⅝ c wine
3 beaten eggs	

Put the lard on ice till it is firm. Take 2 T of it and cut into the flour. Add the eggs, salt, and wine to form a dough. Knead it till it blisters. Cool it ½ hour. Roll thin and dot it all over with the lard. Fold the side edges together and the top and bottom to the center to form an envelope. Roll thin again. Cool ½ hour. Dot with lard and repeat this process till all the lard is used (about 4 times). The last time, brush the dough with beaten egg yolk. Cut in shapes and bake in a hot oven 15-20 minutes.

These biscuits will rise in flakes, will be very tender, fine with luncheon.

Makes about 3 dozen.

COLD YEASTY DOUGH

1 c egg yolks	1 T water
1 c melted shortening	2 T sugar
1 c milk	½ t salt
1 cake yeast	8 c flour

Mix the first 3. Add the yeast softened in the water. Add the rest to form a stiff dough. Tie it in a cloth and place it in a bowl of cold water. Let it stand till the dough bag comes to the surface. Knead, adding more flour if necessary. Let rise till double in bulk. Roll thin on a floured board. This is now ready to use as the basis of any kind of roll or coffee cake. It is rich and "eggy". Here are some suggestions:

Emperor coffee cake.—Put the dough 2 inches thick in the bottom of a large, round, greased baking pan. Cover it with ¼ c chopped, unblanched almonds, ¼ c sugar, ½ t cinnamon, and ⅓ c chopped raisins. Cover this with another layer of dough. Let rise till double and bake in a hot oven 10 minutes and a moderate 30-40 more.

Makes 3 large cakes.

Fine coffee cake.—Add 1 grated lemon rind. Cover the bottom of a greased, round baking pan with chopped almonds (unblanched) and fine bread crumbs. Put the dough on top and let rise till double in bulk. Sprinkle with sugar. Bake in a hot oven 10 minutes and a moderate about 30 more.

Makes 3 large coffee cakes.

Nut tart.—Roll the dough thin. Line odd-shaped tart tins (muffin tins will do) with the dough. Fill ⅔ full with filling as suggested on p. 177, crispy yeasty dough. Cover with another thin layer of dough, but do not have the tart shape full, as they rise. Let rise till double in bulk. Brush with beaten egg yolk and sprinkle with sugar. Bake in a hot oven about 30 minutes.

Makes 5 dozen.

Sour cherry coffee cake.—Put dough 1-inch thick in a greased loaf pan. Cover with sour cherries and plenty of sugar. Cover with another inch of dough and let rise till double in bulk. Bake in a hot oven 10 minutes and a moderate 30 more.

Makes 3 large cakes.

Mrs. Rose Tulea, Cleveland, Ohio

CREAMED OR KNEADED YEASTY DOUGH

½ c butter (sweet preferred)	6 c flour
4 beaten egg yolks	1 cake yeast
2 T sugar	1 T milk
½ c cream	2 beaten egg whites

Cream the butter and add the next 4 ingredients. Add the yeast softened in the milk. Add the egg whites, and blend all to a dough. Knead. Let rise till double in bulk. Knead again and use as the basis of the following:

Almond bread.—Put dough 1-inch thick in greased loaf pans. Brush with beaten egg white. Sprinkle heavily with chopped, unblanched almonds, and sugar. Let rise till double in bulk and bake in a moderate oven about 30 minutes.

Makes 2 loaves.

Coffee ring.—Use sour cream in the creamed yeasty dough, above, instead of sweet. Add ½ c chopped raisins. Divide the dough in 3 parts. Twist these together to form a twisted ring. Pinch the edges together and place on a large, round, greased pan. Brush with beaten egg yolk. Strew with chopped, unblanched almonds and sugar. Let rise till double in bulk, and bake in a hot oven 10 minutes and a moderate 30 more.

Makes 1 large ring.

Hornets' nests.—Roll the dough as thin as paper. Cut strips 4 by 8 inches. Spread with any kind of jam, or poppy seeds, or chopped almonds. Dot with butter. Roll and place, with the cut sides just touching in a greased, deep-sided pan. Sprinkle with sugar and let rise till double. Bake in a moderate oven 25-30 minutes.

Makes 1½ dozen.

Yeasty buns.—Roll ½-inch thick. Cut in squares. Brush with beaten egg yolk and sprinkle with sugar and cinnamon. Let rise till double in bulk. Bake in a hot oven about 20 minutes.

Makes about 2 dozen.

Mrs. Rose Tulea, Cleveland, Ohio

CRISPY YEASTY DOUGH

½ c butter	2 T sugar
3 c flour	¼ t salt
3 egg yolks	1 cake yeast
6 T sour cream	1 T water

Work the butter into the flour. Add the egg yolks and cream. Mix well. Add the rest in order, the yeast having been softened in the water. Let rise 1 hour. Roll thin. Spread very lightly with butter. Fold the sides over to the center and the ends to the center, envelope fashion. Roll thin. Fold again and roll thin. Cut in shapes and put on an ungreased (these are very rich) baking sheet 2 inches apart. Let rise 1 hour. Brush lightly with beaten egg white, and bake in a moderately hot oven 20-30 minutes.

VARIATIONS

This dough may be used in a variety of ways. Small shapes may be put together with filling between. The dough may be rolled thin, covered with filling, and rolled as for jelly roll; cut in pieces and baked as pin wheels; or triangles of dough may be spread with filling and rolled from the wide to the narrow end to form horns or crescents. Brush with beaten egg white and sprinkle with anise or poppy seed. Here are some fillings to use with this dough.

FILLINGS

Cheese

2 c cottage cheese	1 grated lemon rind
½ t salt	½ c raisins
3 beaten eggs	1 T sugar (optional)

Mix in order to a stiff paste.

Prune

2 c chopped, cooked prunes	½ t cinnamon
1 grated lemon rind	2 T sugar

Mix in order to a stiff paste.

Raisin

1 c sugar	1 lemon rind, grated
2 c water	½ t cinnamon
1 c raisins (any chopped, dried fruit)	1 c chopped nuts (optional)

Boil the sugar and water 10 minutes. Add the rest and cook till thick. Cool.

Makes about 2 dozen.

Mrs. Rose Tulea, Cleveland, Ohio

DOUGHNUTS

1 c milk	6 beaten egg yolks
¼ c shortening	1 cake yeast
3 T sugar	1 T water
½ t salt	4 c flour

Scald the milk. Add the next 3 ingredients and cool. Add the eggs, the yeast mixed with the water, and the flour. Knead well

for 5 minutes. Roll ½-inch thick. Cut in doughnuts. Let rise till double in bulk. Fry in hot fat till brown on both sides. (See p. 62.) Drain on brown paper. Sprinkle with sugar.

These are the popular Hungarian doughnuts with the white stripe around the middle. They are very tasty and not at all greasy. For variation, make the dough into twists about 4 inches long,

HUNGARIAN DOUGHNUTS

and fry as above.

Makes about 3 dozen.

FLAKY PASTRY DOUGH

2 c flour	¼ t salt
1 beaten egg	½ cake yeast
2 T sour cream	¼ c water
1 T white wine	1 c butter (preferably sweet)

Mix the first 5 ingredients and add the yeast softened in the water. Knead until small bubbles form on the surface of the dough. Roll out ¼-inch thick. Place the butter on the dough. Fold the dough all over the butter. Sprinkle with flour, and roll and beat the dough till it is flat. Fold the 4 corners envelope fashion and roll thin again. Repeat 4 times. This is now ready for any of the following, or any other shape or filling you prefer. The dough is flaky and rich, so the pans need not be greased.

Almond cake.—Roll thin and line a baking pan. Fill with ½ c raisins, 3 T sugar, 3 T ground, unblanched almonds, ½ grated lemon rind, 3 beaten eggs, all mixed together. Cover this with another layer of dough. Brush with beaten egg yolk and more ground almonds. Let rise till double in bulk. Bake in a moderate oven 30-40 minutes. This is very rich and flaky. Serve with coffee.

Cream patties.—Roll the dough as thin as possible. Cut in rounds. Cut doughnutlike holes in the centers of half the rounds. Brush the plain rounds with beaten egg white. Put on top of each plain round either a doughnut-shaped piece or the small round from the hole of the doughnut. Let rise till double in bulk. Fill the ones with holes with a spoonful of filling made of 4 stiffly beaten egg whites mixed with 1 T sugar and 1 T jam. Bake in a moderate oven 20-30 minutes. This makes an interesting and good patty, rich enough for dessert.

PASTRY VARIATIONS

Makes 1½ dozen.

Flaky folds.—Roll dough in a thin piece 8 inches wide and quite long. Cover with jam or ground nuts. Fold the sides over, pinching the edges together. Brush with beaten egg yolk and let rise on an ungreased pan until double in bulk. Bake in a moderate oven about 30-40 minutes.
Makes about 2 folds.

Horns.—Roll dough thin and cut in triangles. Brush with sugar and melted butter or any kind of filling. Roll in horns.

Sprinkle with sugar and let rise till double in bulk. Bake in a moderate oven about 20-30 minutes.

Pretzels.—Shape thin strips of dough in pretzel pieces. Brush with egg white, and sprinkle with sugar. Let rise till double in bulk and bake in a moderate oven about 15-20 minutes.

Nut slices.—Roll the dough ½-inch thick. Line a baking pan with it. Fill with a mixture of 8 stiffly beaten egg whites, 1 c sugar, ¼ t cloves. Cover with walnut halves. Bake in a moderate oven about 40 minutes or until the top of the loaf is dry and firm.

Mrs. Rose Tulea, Cleveland, Ohio

FRUIT BREAD

12 eggs	2 c chopped raisins
3 c sugar	2 c chopped walnuts
6 c flour	1 c chopped candied peel
2 T B.P.	

Beat the eggs and sugar 1 hour (10 minutes in an electric mixer). Fold in the flour and B.P. sifted together. Add the fruit floured slightly with extra flour. Bake in a greased loaf pan in a slow oven 1 hour.

This is a sweet, fruity loaf that keeps a long time, a month or more, and is fine sliced thin and put together in sandwiches with butter mixed with orange juice, grated lemon, or orange rind.

Makes 3 loaves.

Mrs. Rose Tulea, Cleveland, Ohio

SPAETZEL

1 c milk	1 T water
2 T butter	5 beaten egg yolks
1 T sugar	5 c flour
½ t salt	almonds, raisins, cinna-
1 cake yeast	mon, C. sugar

Scald the milk and add the next 3 ingredients. Cool. Soften the yeast in the water and add. Add 2 c of the flour and mix well. Let rise till light and foamy. Add the eggs and the rest of the flour, and knead well. Let rise till double in bulk. Punch down. Line a greased baking pan with ground, unblanched almonds and bread crumbs sprinkled lightly. Roll the dough thin. Cut round, cookie-shaped pieces. Dip them in melted butter. Lay them in the mold, overlapping. Strew with ground almonds, raisins, cinnamon, and sugar. Put in another layer of dough cookies. Sprinkle again. Continue until there are 4 layers. Let rise till double in bulk, and bake in a hot oven 10 minutes and a moderate 40 more. Brush the top with melted butter.

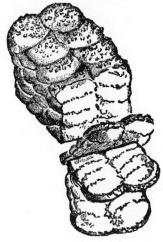

Makes 2 loaves.

SOUR-CREAM SPAETZEL

Substitute sour cream for the milk. Use jam between the layers instead of the filling suggested. Both of these are delicious sliced, for breakfast.

SPAETZEL

Makes 2 loaves.

Mrs. Rose Tulea, Cleveland, Ohio

TWIST

2 T sugar	4 c milk
1 cake yeast	3 beaten egg yolks
2 T lukewarm milk	1 c melted butter
½ t salt	12 c flour

Mix the first 3 and add the rest to form a dough. Knead. Let rise till double in bulk. Knead again. Divide the dough into long, thick ribbons. Twist 2 together to form a twisted loaf.

Let rise on a greased baking pan till double in bulk. Brush with melted butter and bake in a hot oven 10 minutes and a moderate 40 more. If small twists are made, bake in a hot oven 15-20 minutes.

Makes 3 loaves.

Mrs. Rose Tulea, Cleveland, Ohio

TWISTED FRUIT BREAD

4 c chopped fruit such as dates, prunes, etc.	1 c grated chocolate
⅔ c quince or other stiff jelly	2 c chopped nuts

Add this mixture to the recipe for twists. Shape into long loaves and place in a greased baking pan. Let rise till double in bulk. Bake in a hot oven 10 minutes and a moderate 50 more.

This makes a most delicious, fruity bread, fine at any time.

Makes 4 large loaves.

Mrs. Rose Tulea, Cleveland, Ohio

ZWIEBACK

Use the twist dough (p. 181), omitting ½ c of the shortening. Shape into a long loaf wider at both ends than in the middle (this is a characteristic of Hungarian zwieback). Let rise till double in bulk on a greased pan. Bake in a hot oven 10 minutes and a moderate 50 more. Brush with egg white and return to the oven 1 minute. Cool. Cut in inch-wide pieces and return them to a moderate oven to dry out. They should be crisp and crumby.

Makes 3 loaves.

Mrs. Rose Tulea, Cleveland, Ohio

INDIA

Indian bread is close to the earliest type of bread in that it is unleavened and baked in cracker form on griddles. The Indians have a careful grading of flour; *soojee* or *relong* is like semolina; *alta* is a whole-meal flour, and *mydah* is like the best pastry flour. All of these recipes originally called for *ghee,* a kind of oil made from buffalo or cow butter. It is free from impurities and will boil without deteriorating or sputtering. For the American who wants to try these just for fun, ordinary butter does quite well. With a combination of flour, ghee, and water or coconut milk, the Indian makes a dough from which he shapes crackers called by many names, most common of which is chuppaties. These are eaten every day, and it is said that the lady, and sometimes the man, of the house takes a great deal of pride in making them.

Most people do not care much for the unleavened bread of India because they are thinking of our light breads and do not see how a cracker, or "petrified pancake" as someone called it, can be bread. If you want to do something very different in the way of a meal, look up a good curry recipe and the rest of the dishes that go with it, make some chuppaties, invite some broad-minded guests with gourmet tastes, and you'll have a different meal that is different.

CHUPPATIES (Wheat Cakes)

1 c white flour
1 c whole-wheat flour
½ t salt

2 T ghee (melted butter)
½ c water

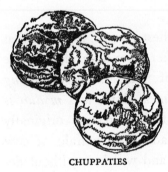

CHUPPATIES

Mix to a dough and let stand 1 hour. Knead well. Make balls of bits of dough and flatten them out thin and round. Bake on a slightly greased griddle over a slow fire, turning them again and again until they are evenly browned but not hard. Regrease the griddle for each baking.

These may be varied by the addition of 3 T B. sugar.

Makes about 1 dozen.

PARATTAS (White-Flour Cakes)

2 c pastry flour
¼ c melted butter

½ t salt
½ c water

Mix to a soft dough and knead till pliable. Form into a long roll 1-inch in diameter and cut off 1-inch pieces. Flatten them down and brush with melted butter. Put 6 together in this way and roll out very thin to the size of a plate. Bake on a slightly greased skillet over a slow fire 10 minutes on each side; turn only once.

These are good with salads, as they are like a flaky cracker.

Makes about 10.

POTATO PURIS

1 c mashed potato   ¼ t salt
1 c flour

Mix and roll as thin as possible. Cut in cakes as large as a saucer. Bake on greased griddle over a slow fire till brown on both sides. Serve without butter.

Fine with a meal of curry.

Makes about 5.

RICE-AND-COCONUT BREAD

4 c rice flour   ½ c B. sugar
½ c desiccated coconut 1½ c boiling water (or coco-
            nut milk)

Mix to a stiff dough. Roll thin, and cut in large, flat rounds. This is difficult but possible. Bake on a greased griddle, over a slow fire till brown on both sides. Turn only once.

These have the grittiness of rice flour and are liked by those who appreciate that flavor and texture. Good with curry or salads.

Makes about 6.

RICE-FLOUR CHUPPATIES

1 c rice flour   ⅓ c water
¼ t salt

Mix to a dough. Take small pieces and flatten to round, thin cakes. Bake on a greased griddle over a slow fire till brown on both sides.

These are very gritty. Barley or fine oatmeal may be substituted and the cakes made thicker.

All of the recipes in this section were developed from suggestions given by *Mrs. Florence Martin Andrews,* Columbus, Ohio, who spent her girlhood in Burma.

Makes about 18.

IRELAND

Ireland, whether she believes it or not, is much like the rest of the British Isles in her bread likes and dislikes. The recipes for ordinary white bread and scones are so similar that we have not included them. But there are some characteristic things like the soda bread, the gingerbread, and the potato pancake that the good old individual Irish, with a bit of this and that, have stamped indelibly as their own.

BARM BRACK BREAD

1 cake yeast	5 c flour
1/4 c water	1 1/2 c currants
1 c milk	1 grated lemon rind
1/2 c melted shortening	1 t salt
3 beaten eggs	1/3 c chopped, candied peel
2/3 c sugar	

Soften the yeast in the water and add the next 5 ingredients. Let rise till double in bulk. Add the rest of the ingredients. Mix well. Put in a well-greased loaf pan and let rise 1 hour.

Bake in a hot oven 10 minutes and a moderate 50 more. Brush the top with melted butter.

This bread is attributed to Lady Gregory, and it is said that William Butler Yeats called this "freckle bread." It is very good served with a St. Patrick's Day luncheon.

Makes 2 loaves.

Mrs. Mary Lintner Lewis,
Rio Grande, Ohio

BARM BRACK BREAD

POTATO PANCAKES

1 c mashed potato	2 beaten eggs
2 c flour	1 c milk
1 t salt	4 T light corn syrup
3 t B.P.	1 T nutmeg

Mix to a batter. Beat well. Bake on a greased griddle till brown on both sides.

These have an excellent flavor. Do not expect them to be like the American variety of pancakes.

Makes about 1 dozen.

GINGERBREAD

½ c shortening	1½ t soda
¼ c sugar	1 t allspice
½ c dark corn syrup	¼ t salt
1 beaten egg	¼ c chopped, blanched
1 egg yolk	almonds
3 c flour	⅓ c chopped peel
1½ t ginger	¼ c raisins
	½ c buttermilk or sour milk

Cream the shortening and sugar; add the syrup, egg, and sifted-together, dry ingredients to which the fruit and peel have been added. Add the milk, and blend. Bake in a greased loaf pan in a moderately slow oven 1 hour. This is not like our idea of gingerbread, but a fruity, spicy loaf, fine for thin, tea sandwiches.

Makes 1 loaf.

Mary Doyle, Cleveland, Ohio

FRUIT BREAD

4½ c flour	1 c raisins
2 t salt	1 c currants
2 T sugar	2 T caraway seeds
3 T B.P. (this is not too	(optional)
much)	2 c milk
½ c shortening	

Cut the shortening into the sifted-together, dry ingredients. Add the rest in order. Mix well. Bake in a greased loaf pan in a slow oven about 1 hour. It is traditional to use a heavy, iron frying pan. Do not try to slice this till it is cold.

It is a good fruity loaf.

Makes 2 medium loaves.

Mary Doyle, Cleveland, Ohio

FRUIT SODA BREAD

4 c flour	1 c sugar
1 t soda	1 c raisins
1 t salt	1 t caraway seed
¾ c shortening	1⅓ c buttermilk

Cut the shortening into the sifted-together, dry ingredients. Add the rest in order. Mix well. Bake in a greased baking pan in a moderate oven 1 hour. This type of bread is sometimes called "singin' hinnie" in England. This recipe was contributed by *Cecelia M. Daly,* a little girl who won the Girl Scouts' cookie baking contest in New York City recently. It is her mother's recipe.

Makes 2 loaves.

Mrs. J. Daly, New York City

SODA BREAD

SODA MIXTURE

1 t sugar	1 t B.P.
1 t soda	1 t salt

Sift and keep on hand for this bread.

DOUGH

1 c flour	½ c sour milk
1½ t soda mixture	

Mix to a soft dough. Bake in a well-greased pan in a hot oven 10-12 minutes. Substitute ⅔ c whole-wheat flour for ⅔ c of the white, for brown soda bread.

This bread is supposed to be broken, not cut, and served hot for tea. It is a traditional Irish bread.

Makes 1 loaf.

Mrs. Mary Lintner Lewis, Rio Grande, Ohio

ITALY

Italy, being a wine country and not having yeast from brewing to depend on, early developed recipes that use eggs for the leavening agent rather than yeast. There are yeast breads, of course; witness the round, hard loaf so common in Italy, so well known to the traveler, and so universally enjoyed by the native. Such a valuable leavening agent could not long remain unknown. But the breads made with the use of many eggs are an interesting characteristic of this country. They have been a bit difficult for the beginner to make, what with all that long beating, but modern mixers take care of that trouble.

The special breads made for feast days are interesting features of Italy's breadbasket. They call for many unusual ingredients, such as malaga pulp, piñon nuts, and chestnut flour, but, for most people, the effort to secure these things is justified in the loaf. For a very special treat, try the pannetone di natale, a world famous Christmas loaf chuck full of fruits, nuts, and peels, and you'll want the holiday season to come again soon so that you'll have a good excuse to make more of this delicious bread.

BREAD OR ROLLS

2 c warm water	2 beaten eggs
1 cake yeast	1 T melted lard
2 t salt	8 c flour

Mix in order and let stand 5 hours. Add enough more flour to make a dough that will knead. Knead well. Form long loaves pointed at the end. Let rise on a greased baking sheet till double in bulk. Bake in a hot oven 10 minutes and a moderate 50 more.

To make rolls, add ½ c melted butter. Shape into large, crescent shapes, using corn meal on the board when you roll the dough, and sprinkle corn meal over them. Let rise till double in bulk and bake in a hot oven about 20 minutes.

These are excellent with breakfast coffee or chocolate.

Makes 2 large loaves or about 4 dozen rolls.

Mrs. Gilda Cassasanda, Columbus, Ohio

CHESTNUT FRUIT BREAD

½ c ground chestnuts or walnuts	⅓ c chopped raisins
½ c ground, blanched almonds	⅓ c ground figs
⅓ c currants	1 c chestnut flour (white flour will do)
	½ c wine or brandy

Mix to a stiff dough, using a little more wine if necessary. Knead till it will hold together. Put in a round baking pan well greased with olive oil. Brush the top with olive oil and bake in a slow oven 1-1½ hours.

This makes a very solid, fruity loaf that has a wonderful flavor with just a slight tang of olive oil, and will keep very well. It is popular in the north of Italy where there are many chestnuts.

Makes 1 loaf.

CRISPITELL

½ c flour	⅛ t salt
2 beaten egg yolks	water (if needed for stiff dough)

Mix to a noodlelike dough. Cut in strips 1-inch wide. Fry in hot fat as for doughnuts. Serve at once.

These are good with coffee or cold milk. They are often served at Christmas time. If they are made in long pencil form they are called "rusp"; if in short pencil form, "struffle."

Makes about 1 dozen.

Mrs. Carmella Peppe, Columbus, Ohio

LIGURIAN BREAD

2 cakes yeast	1 t salt
1 c flour	½ c grape pulp (jam may be used)
½ c water	
⅓ c softened butter	½ c piñon nuts (others may be substituted)
½ c sugar	
3 beaten egg yolks	3–4 c flour

Mix the first 3 ingredients and let stand till bubbly. Add the rest in order and knead. Let rise till almost double in bulk. Shape into a round loaf. Cut a cross on the top and let rise on a greased pan till double in bulk. Bake in a moderate oven 1-1½ hours.

This is a solid bread with an odd taste and color from the grape. It takes a long time to rise, but it will keep well. For an extra touch, brush it with egg white, stick piñon nuts all over the top, and return to the oven for 5 minutes.

Makes 1 large loaf.

MONK'S BREAD

1 c sugar	½ c finely chopped citron
7 eggs	⅝ c flour (½ c + 2 T)
2 squares melted chocolate	1 t cinnamon
½ c ground, unblanched almonds	¼ t cloves

Beat the sugar and eggs until very light and fluffy. Add the rest in order. Pour ½ inch thick and bake in greased shallow pan in a moderate oven 30-40 minutes.

Serve cold cut in squares, for tea.

Makes 1 loaf.

NEAPOLITAN BREAD

1 c ground, blanched almonds
4 beaten egg yolks
1 beaten egg

1½ c butter
1 grated lemon rind
2 c C. sugar
3¼ c cake flour

Mix all to a paste, kneading hard and long. Chill 1 hour before using. With the hands, make thin ribbons, using extra flour if necessary. Braid 3 together, cutting the braid about 6 inches long. Brush with beaten egg yolks. Bake on a greased baking sheet in a moderate oven about 20-30 minutes. Watch, as they burn easily. Or add 1 grated orange rind and 1 well-beaten egg. Put in greased loaf pan and bake in a moderate oven about 45 minutes.

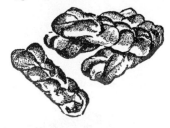

NEAPOLITAN BREAD

This is very sweet, fragile, and cakelike. It should be served only with tea or at an evening party with a beverage.

Makes 2 loaves.

NEAPOLITAN EASTER BREAD

Use for the dough half the bread recipe of Mrs. Cassasanda (p. 191), omitting ½ c water and using ½ c egg yolks instead. Line a greased pie pan with the risen dough, rolled ½-inch thick. Fill it with 3 c of filling made by grinding together whatever you happen to have on hand of such things as cooked smoked ham, salami, bacon (ordinary or Canadian) cooked sausage, cheese, parsley, a bit of onion and garlic, or any pre-

pared meat such as bologna. Cover the top with a thin layer
of dough, pinching the edges as for piecrust. Brush with beaten
egg yolk. Let rise till double in bulk and bake in hot oven 10
minutes and a moderate about 40 more.

This is a very flavorful bread, good hot or cold with salad
luncheons.

Makes 1 loaf.

Mrs. *Carmella Peppe*, Columbus, Ohio

PANNETONE DI NATALE

2 cakes yeast
½ c milk
½ c flour
1½ c shortening
1 c sugar
3 beaten egg yolks
6 beaten eggs

1 t vanilla
8 c flour
1 t salt
1 c raisins
½ c chopped, candied peel
¼ c chopped citron
¼ c chopped almonds

PANNETONE DI NATALE

Mix the yeast, milk, and
½ c flour. Let stand till light
and bubbly. Cream the sugar
and shortening. Add the
eggs. Add this to the yeast
mixture and add the rest in
order. Knead. Let rise till
double in bulk. Knead again
and shape into round loaves.
Put in greased baking pans
and let rise till double in
bulk. This will take some time because of the fruit. Bake in
a hot oven 10 minutes and a moderate 50 more.

This may be baked in a tube pan, the bottom of which is
covered with whole almonds and a sprinkle of sugar. Or the
fruit may be mixed with only ½ the dough, the plain dough
rolled out, and the fruited dough covered with the plain. When
this is baked and sliced, there will be a layer of dough surrounding a fruity middle.

This is the famous Italian Christmas bread that is so popular at holiday time. It is delicious with a beverage, and, like all holiday breads, keeps well enough so that it may be on hand during the season.

Makes 2 loaves.

PITTSEKIN

Use for the dough half the bread recipe of Mrs. Cassasanda (p. 191). Put it 1-inch thick in a deep-sided, greased pan. With

PITTSEKIN

a sharp knife slash the top ½-inch deep crisscross fashion. On each square put a very thin slice of onion with a little piece of garlic on top. Cover the whole thing with the solid part of canned tomatoes. Let rise till double in bulk. Bake in a hot oven 10 minutes and a moderate 40 more.

Excellent with a salad luncheon.

Makes 1 loaf.

Mrs. Carmella Peppe, Columbus, Ohio

POLENTA

½ c corn meal
2 c boiling water
½ t salt

⅛ t paprika
½ c grated cheese

Stir the meal gradually into the salted water. Cook over the direct flame, stirring constantly, as it burns easily. After 10 minutes, cook over water (double boiler) 1 hour. Stir in the cheese and paprika. Put in a dish or pan till it is cold and stiff. Slice and fry in olive oil till brown on both sides. Serve plain or with highly seasoned tomato sauce.

While this may not seem like bread, it is used extensively by Italians, especially the lower classes, in place of bread. Sometimes it is eaten as a mush before the molding and frying.
Makes 1 loaf.

Mrs. Josephine de Tirro Baker, Columbus, Ohio

SIENESE GINGERBREAD

1 c honey	½ t ginger
½ c chopped, unblanched almonds	⅛ lb. grated, sweet chocolate
	½ t B.P.
2 T chopped peel	¾ c rye flour
⅛ t cinnamon	½ c white flour

Warm the honey. Add the rest in order. Bake in a greased loaf pan in a moderate oven about 30 minutes. Sprinkle with sugar while still warm.

This is an unusual gingerbread, with the combination of rye and sweet chocolate giving it a fine flavor. It is good with tea.
Makes 1 loaf.

SPICE BREAD

1½ c shortening	½ t mace
4 c C. sugar	1 t soda
9 well-beaten egg yolks	½ t salt
1½ t cinnamon	3½ c flour
½ t allspice	1½ c sour cream
1 t nutmeg	9 stiffly beaten egg whites

Cream the shortening and sugar. Add the egg yolks. Add the sifted-together, dry ingredients alternately with the cream. Fold in the egg whites. Bake in a greased loaf pan in a moderate oven 1 hour.

This has a texture like pound cake and a wonderfully spicy flavor.
Makes 1 large loaf.

SWEET BREAD

1 c shortening	2 c flour
¾ c sugar	½ t B.P.
6 eggs	1 c chopped, candied peel

Cream the shortening and sugar. Add the eggs 2 at a time, beating well after each addition. Sift the B.P. with the flour and add. Mix well. Bake in a long, narrow, greased pan, a layer of dough, a layer of fruit, etc., until the fruit is all used. Bake in a moderately hot oven about 40 minutes.

This is a rich tea bread, full of fruit and very "eggy."

Makes 1 loaf.

TORTONA

Use for the dough half the recipe of Mrs. Cassasanda's bread (p. 191). With pencil-like strips of dough, form figure 8's, leaving half of the top part of the 8 off: ∝ . Place a hard-cooked egg at the place where the dough is crossed. Let rise till double in bulk. As the dough rises it will partially embed the egg. Brush with beaten egg yolk. Bake in a hot oven 20-30 minutes.

These odd rolls are served at Eastertime. They are fine for the Easter breakfast.

Makes about 2 dozen.

Mrs. Carmella Peppe, Columbus, Ohio

# MEXICO

With the great interest we are showing for travel in Mexico, it is no wonder that our travelers come back with an enthusiasm for Mexican meals and a desire to have a Mexican party with real Mexican food. While not like our usual idea of bread, the tortilla is the Mexican staff of life; in fact, not only the staff of life but, with the ancients and less well-to-do moderns, the knife, fork, and spoon as well. So, whether you're serving your own interpretation of *almuerzo* (elaborate breakfast), *comida* (midday dinner), *merienda* (afternoon meal), or *cena* (late evening meal), you'll want to have the tortillas of one kind or another in order to do the right thing. If you have *desayuno,* or early morning coffee, you won't need the tortilla, as this is the only time when that bread does not appear. You will, however, want to have the pan dulce, a delicious sweet bun, traditional with morning coffee.

With the exception of the use of better implements, the making of the tortilla has changed very little in the past four hundred years, as we can tell from a description of the process given by one of Cortez' men: "To make the bread they build a fire under a large jug; when the water boils, they take the fire away and put some grain in the jug and they add a little lime to make the skin loosen. Later they wash it well, and they grind it on stones shaped for that purpose. While grinding it they throw water on it, and it becomes a paste."

You'll have more fun making tortillas by the modern method, but you'll turn out a product like that described by Cortez.

BUÑUELOS *

one 2″ piece stick cinnamon	1 T lard
1 c water	⅛ t salt
1 T sugar	½ c sugar
1 beaten egg yolk	one 5″ piece stick cinnamon
3½ c flour	

Boil the 2-inch piece of cinnamon in the water until it is slightly colored. Drain. While it is warm, add the T of sugar. Mix the egg yolk with the flour and the lard until blended. Add the first mixture to this a little at a time until the mass is well blended. Add the salt. Wrap the dough in a cloth and place in a covered pan in a cool place for 2 hours. Roll very thin, using more flour if necessary. The Mexican cook rolls it over her bare knee to make it thinner and crisper. Cut in desired shapes and fry in lard as for doughnuts. Drain on brown paper. Dust in the sugar mixed with the 5-inch piece of cinnamon, ground.

These are much like sweet crackers.

Makes about 3 dozen.

BUÑOCHUELOS *

⅓ c shortening	½ c flour
½ c sugar	⅛ t cinnamon
1 beaten egg yolk	¼ t salt
⅓ c corn meal	

Cream the sugar and shortening. Add the rest in order. Roll thin. Cut in small doughnut shapes. Or take tiny pieces of dough and make in rings by winding once around the little finger. Bake on a greased baking sheet in a moderate oven 5-10 minutes. Dust with sugar.

These are "little buñuelos," called so because they are very light, thin, and airy. Persons who have done things in a hurry and without thought are asked, "E buñochuelo?"—"Do you think it is nothing?"

Makes about 1 dozen.

CORN MEAL TORTILLAS

1 c corn meal	⅔ t salt
1 c boiling water	

Slowly add the water to the meal. Add the salt. Shape in thin, flat cakes and bake on an ungreased griddle till they are brown on both sides.

These are much like the thin southern corn pones.

Makes 4.

GALLETAS (Crackers) *

4 c flour	2 t melted butter or lard
1 t B.P.	1¼ c milk or thin cream
2 t salt	2 beaten eggs

Mix in order, to form dough. Roll thin. Cut into crackers and bake on a greased baking sheet in a hot oven 5-8 minutes.

These are good and crisp. Serve them with salads or Mexican meals.

Makes about 4 dozen.

MILK TORTILLAS

½ c lard and butter mixed   ½ t salt
2 c flour   6 T milk (about)

Cut the shortening into the flour and salt. Use only enough milk to hold the mass together. Make little balls. Flatten them out thin on a floured board. Bake on a hot, ungreased griddle till they are brown on both sides.

Makes about 1½ dozen.

PAN DE HUEVO (Egg Bread) *

12 egg yolks   1 T water
½ c sugar   3 T aniseed
2 T melted lard   12 stiffly beaten egg whites
2 cakes yeast   3½ c flour

Beat the egg yolks till thick and lemon colored. Add the sugar slowly and continue to beat. Add the lard, and the yeast dissolved in the water. Add the rest in order. Let rise till double in bulk. Knead down. Roll ½-inch thick, using a little more flour if necessary. Cut in large squares and put on greased pans to rise double in bulk. Bake in a hot oven 10 minutes and a moderate 40 more.

This is very "eggy," a good breakfast bread.

Makes 2 loaves.

PAN DULCE (Sweet Bread) *

1 T sugar   ½ t salt
2 cakes yeast   1½ c sugar
1½ c warm water   2 T melted shortening
2 c flour   4 beaten eggs
   3 c flour

Mix the sugar, yeast and water. Add the flour and salt. Let this rise till double in bulk. Add the rest in order, and knead. Let rise till double in bulk. Knead on board, using 1 more c of flour if necessary. With the hands, form small, round buns. Ice and let rise on a greased pan till double in bulk. Place in a moderate oven 30 minutes.

ICING

1½ c flour	½ c shortening
1 c sugar	¼ c cream
1 beaten egg	1 t cinnamon

Mix to a paste that will spread.

These are delicious sweet buns that are served for the desayuno, first breakfast, in Mexico.

Makes about 4 dozen.

TORTILLAS *

1 c finely ground, cooked	1 T corn meal
hominy (masa)	2 T water

Add the corn meal and water to the hominy paste, and mix till smooth. Take bits of dough and roll with the hands to form flat biscuit about ½-inch in diameter and ½-inch thick. Dif-

TORTILLAS

ficult but possible. Put them on a moist cloth on a breadboard. Cover with another moist cloth and a second board. Exert even pressure on the tortillas until they are wafer thin. Bake on a very hot, ungreased griddle until they are slightly brown on both sides. Carefully remove and keep warm between cloths until used.

The tortilla tostada, one that has been put in a slow oven for crisping, is more popular with Americans. These are like crackers until they are covered, but the limp kind is the proper kind. Serve with any Mexican meal.

In the olden days, the masa (or *nixtamal*, as it was called) was made by soaking corn in lye till the husk came off and grinding it on stones, or *metates*, throwing more water on all the while to make a paste. The tortillas were shaped at once from the moist dough; the whole process took about 8 hours.

Makes about 1 dozen.

QUESADILLAS (Cheese Cakes) *

1 c masa (see tortilla recipe above)	⅔ c grated cheese 1 t salt

Mix the masa with ½ the cheese and salt. Divide the dough into 18 parts. Make into flat cakes. Put a little cheese in the center of each. Bring the sides together and pinch. Fry in lard, as doughnuts. Difficult to make, but good.

These are fine with green salads.

Makes 1½ dozen.

---

* All recipes marked by the star, as well as the historical material, are adapted from McNeil, Blanche and Edna, *First Foods of America*, Suttonhouse Ltd., Los Angeles, California.

RUSSIA

The black bread of Russia is a tradition in fact as well as in the fancy of literature. Like most of the European peasant breads, it is sour and solid, but it has a heavy charm of its own and has nourished millions. Contrast this black bread with the marvelous holiday loaf characteristic of Russia and all other Slavic countries. Here is a loaf made of the best things the housewife can find. Full of fruit and flavor, it is a delight to the eye as well as the stomach.

The basis of Russian cooking is said to be sour cream. Certainly we find that lavish use is made of it in the breads. The blini could not be made without it, and many of the fillings for that peculiarly Russian delicacy require it.

Many are the traditions and superstitions connected with bread in Russia. No peasant likes to stay in a house where there is no bread, "for how can he who forgets the gift of God expect divine protection?" People who waste bread will be weighed on judgment day and their weight compared to that of the pieces of bread they have wasted. If the wasted bread outweighs the person, he is lost to Satan. At the time of harvest, bread is blessed by the priest to make the grain grow, and loaves are placed near the seed, or bits of bread are put into the ground with the seed, to insure a good harvest. Particularly comforting is this proverb, "Without a bit of bread even a palace is sad, but with it a pine tree is paradise."

BLINI

2½ c milk	2 beaten eggs
½ t salt	½ cake yeast
½ c butter	1 T water
¼ c sugar	5 c flour
½ c sour cream	1½ c rye flour

Scald the milk. Add the next 4 ingredients. Cool. Add the eggs, and the yeast softened in the water. Add the flours and mix well. Let rise 4 hours. Beat well. Bake on a greased griddle in small thin pancakes, over a low fire. Serve these at once with plenty of sour cream, cottage cheese, caviar, smoked salmon, or the filling for cheese rolls (below). White flour may be substituted for the rye in plain blini, and sour milk may be used for the cream. See also Continental Pancakes, p. 238.

Makes about 4 dozen.

CHEESE ROLLS

4 c cottage cheese	1 T sugar (optional)
½ c melted butter	1 t caraway seed (optional)
2 t salt	3 beaten eggs
	1 c sour cream

Mix all together and spread generously on large, split, homemade rolls or rye-bread slices. Put in a moderate oven until the rolls are hot and the filling "set."

These are excellent with salad or at evening with coffee.

Makes 3 dozen.

EASTER BREAD

4 c milk, scalded and cooled	2 c sugar
16 c flour	1 c melted shortening
4 cakes yeast	2 c currants
10 beaten egg yolks	4 T vanilla

Add 6 c flour to the milk. Blend in the yeast. Let rise all night. Next morning, add the rest in order and mix well. Let rise till double in bulk. Knead well, using a little more flour if necessary. Put in greased loaf pans and let rise till double in bulk. Bake 10 minutes in a hot oven and 50 more in a moderate. Brush with beaten egg yolk and return to the oven 1 minute.

This makes a large amount, but it is delicious and will keep well.

Makes 4 large loaves.

SOUR RYE BREAD

½ c lukewarm water	1½ c sour milk
2 cakes yeast	5 c rye flour
1 T sugar	1 c white flour
1 c white flour	½ c whole-wheat flour
2 t salt	

Mix the first 4 ingredients and let stand till bubbly. Add the rest in order and knead well 10 minutes. Let rise till double in bulk. Knead 10 minutes more. Put the dough in a large bowl lined with a well-floured cloth. When it is double in bulk, invert the bowl and let the dough fall carefully on to a greased-and-floured baking sheet. If the cloth has stuck, remove it carefully. Bake in a hot oven 10 minutes and a moderate 100 more.

This makes the traditional round loaf of European countries and allows the loaf to rise more easily while baking because there is no crust on top to slow down the yeast action in this heavy rye dough. Keep ½ the dough from the first baking to add to the next if you want a real "sour rye." Add 2 T caraway seeds if liked. Keep only 2 or 3 days in cool place.

Make 2 loaves.

UKRANIAN EASTER BREAD

For Ukranian Easter Bread, add to the easter bread dough (p. 206) 1 c chopped raisins, 1 c chopped nuts, 1 c chopped, candied peel. In the Lesteshen family this loaf is baked in a big dishpan for hours and is used throughout the Easter season.

Mary Lesteshen, Cleveland, Ohio

SCANDINAVIAN COUNTRIES

NORWAY, SWEDEN, AND DENMARK

Get out your raisins, currants, candied peel, almonds, brown sugar, rye flour, cardamon, anise, caraway, plenty of eggs—in fact, get out all the good things your cupboard holds, for if you're going to make any breads from the Scandinavian countries, you'll need them. Here are sweet tea breads like cake, rings and braids, *limpe* bread with a flavor like no other rye bread, buns and rolls of finest texture, the knackebrød, spisbrød, fladbrød—such a variety of fancy things that you'll want to make them all.

And you'll like them all too, with the possible exception of the various species of knackebrød—really a thin, brittle sheet of rye in cracker form that someone has aptly described as a "victrola record." In the fall, a good housewife bakes a huge supply of these, using rye, barley, ground oats —husk and all—and potato or pea-meal flours in various combinations (the coarser types are reserved for horses), bakes them hard, often on an iron-plate arrangement over an open fire, and then strings them by means of the center hole on a long pole. The pole, holding its precious winter's supply, is stored on racks near the ceiling of the house. The knackebrød should never be eaten until it is at least a week old and is better after three months; and it is said that a certain Swedish archbishop announced that it might keep about twenty years, "and then be only reasonably stale."

Many are the traditions connected with the eating of bread in these Scandinavian countries. For instance, a boy and a girl eating from the same loaf will fall in love. And bread is broken before and after the wedding ceremony, and during the ceremony each guest is given a loaf of bread and a bottle of ale that he must get rid of before he goes home in order to insure the happiness of the young couple.

After trying some of this fine array of breads, we can agree with the Norwegian proverb, "Bread is better than the song of birds."

Denmark

COFFEE CAKE

2 c flour	¼ c sugar
3 t B.P.	2 beaten eggs
½ t salt	¼ c milk
⅓ c shortening	¼ c chopped, seedless raisins

Cut the shortening into the sifted-together, dry ingredients as for pie dough. Mix the sugar and eggs. Add the milk. Make a hole in the center of the flour mixture and pour in the liquids and the raisins. Mix well. Put in a greased loaf pan.

Brush with slightly beaten white of egg. Sprinkle with sugar, ground nuts, and finely chopped citron or grated orange rind. Bake in a hot oven 20-30 minutes.

Makes 1 coffee cake.

FLAKY BUNS WITH VARIATIONS

7 c flour	1½ cakes yeast
½ c sugar	1 T sugar
1¾ c milk	1½ c butter
6-8 cardamon seeds	

FLAKY-BUN VARIATIONS

Mix the sugar and flour. Add the milk and seeds and the yeast softened in the T of sugar. Mix well. Roll ½-inch thick on a floured board. Dot all with butter. Fold the side edges toward the middle and the top and bottom to the middle. Roll again. Dot with butter and continue this process until the butter is all used and well worked in. Let the dough stand in a cold place until firm. Use it as the basis for:

Envelopes.—Roll dough ½-inch thick and cut in 3-inch squares. Spread with a filling of ⅓ c ground almonds, ½ c C. sugar, ¼ c butter blended. Fold the corners to make an envelope and pinch the ends together. Brush with slightly beaten egg and sprinkle with chopped, blanched almonds or hazelnuts. Let rise on a greased pan till double in bulk, and bake in a moderate oven 25-30 minutes.

Flaky kuchen.—Press dough into a square, greased tin 1-inch thick. Make dents in it 1-inch apart and sprinkle thickly with B. sugar, cinnamon, and chopped nuts. Let rise till double in bulk. Bake in a moderate oven about 40 minutes.

This is a very rich, flaky dough like puff pastry. For those who like sweet rolls, there is nothing better for breakfast.

Raspberry buns.—Roll dough 1-inch thick. Cut in large rounds. Make a hole in the middle of each and fill it with raspberry jam. Let rise until double in size on a greased baking sheet. Sprinkle with C. sugar, and bake in a moderate oven 25-30 minutes.

Sweet squares.—Roll dough 1-inch thick. Cut in 2-inch squares. Let rise to twice their size on a greased baking sheet. Bake 25-30 minutes in a moderate oven. Cool. Ice with 1 beaten egg thickened with enough C. sugar to spread, and sprinkle with ground, blanched almonds. Return to oven for 1 minute.

Twists.—Roll the dough ½-inch thick. Cut ½-inch strips and twist 2 together, shaping the twist into rings or figure 8's. Put on greased baking sheet. Brush with lightly beaten egg; sprinkle with finely ground, blanched almonds. Let rise till double in bulk. Bake in a moderately hot oven 25-30 minutes.

Makes about 3 dozen rolls and 2 kuchen.

Norway

JULE KAGE (Christmas Bread)

2 c scalded milk	1 T ground cardamon
1 c sugar	1 c chopped raisins
2 t salt	½ c chopped citron
1 c melted shortening	½ c candied cherries
2 cakes yeast	½ c chopped, blanched
½ c lukewarm water	almonds
	8-9 c flour

Combine the first 4 ingredients. When this is cool, add the yeast, that has been softened in the water. Add 4 c of the flour. Mix well. Let rise till double in bulk. Punch down and add the rest of the ingredients, saving a few pieces of citron and cherries for decoration. Let rise again till double in bulk. This will take a long time because of all the fruit. Punch down, knead again, and put in greased loaf pans. Let rise till double in bulk. Bake in a hot oven 10 minutes and moderate 50 more. Brush with melted butter or cream. Those who prefer it may frost with a thin, C.-sugar-and-water glaze and decorate with the cherries and citron.

This makes a beautiful, traditional Christmas cake. There's nothing better for the Christmas breakfast or afternoon coffee or served in the evening with coffee or wine.

Makes 3 cakes.

Mrs. Sam Cornelius, Cleveland, Ohio

RUGBRØD (Rye Bread)

1 c graham flour	2 c boiling water
3 c rye flour	1 cake yeast
¼ c B. sugar	1 c lukewarm water
1 T salt	5 c flour

Pour the boiling water over the first 4 ingredients. Cool. Mix the yeast with the lukewarm water; add it to the first mixture. Add the white flour to make a stiff dough. Knead. Let rise till double in bulk. Knead again and put in greased loaf pans. Let rise till double in bulk and bake in a hot oven 10 minutes and a moderate 70 more.

This is a good, light rye without the seeds.

Makes 2 large loaves.

Sweden

BEER RYE BREAD

٬2 c water	1 T warm water
1½ c beer	2 t salt
⅔ c Orleans molasses (warmed)	5 c coarse rye flour or meal
1 cake yeast	5 c flour

Mix the first 3 ingredients, and add the yeast softened in the water. Add the rest in order and mix well. Let rise till double in bulk. Knead, using more white flour if necessary. Line a bowl with a floured cloth. Put the dough in on the cloth. Let rise till double in bulk. Carefully turn the risen dough out onto a greased pan, with the part that was *up* in the bowl *down* on the pan. Remove the cloth, and bake in a hot oven 10 minutes and a moderate about 50 more.

This method of rising makes a soft dough on top during the baking process and lets the heavy rye mixture rise better while baking.

Makes about 3 loaves.

Mrs. Russel Squire, Los Angeles, California

FRUIT BREAD

1 cake yeast	½ c chopped English
1 c warm pear or prune	walnuts
juice	½ c chopped almonds
2 c flour	½ c chopped figs
½ c cooked, chopped	1 t cinnamon
prunes	½ t nutmeg
½ c cooked, chopped	¼ t allspice
dried pears (spiced	¼ c brandy
may be used)	1 T wine
1 c raisins	½ c B. sugar
1 c currants	1 t salt
¼ c chopped citron	4-5 c flour

Mix the first 3 ingredients, and let stand 2 hours. Add the rest in order, using only enough flour to make a stiff dough. Let rise till double in bulk. Punch down. Put in greased pans and let rise till double in bulk. Bake 1½ hours in a moderate oven. This is a very fruity bread that keeps well. The recipe has been used in Mrs. Radical's own family for 2 generations before her, and she is now 90.

Makes 2 large loaves.

Mrs. William Radical, Bosler, Wyoming

CORN MEAL BREAD

2 c boiling water	1 cake yeast
1 c corn meal	2 T lukewarm water
2 T shortening	¾ c dark corn syrup
2 t salt	9 c flour

Pour the water over the next 3 ingredients. Cool. Add yeast softened in lukewarm water. Add syrup and flour. Knead until elastic. Let rise till double in bulk. Punch down. Put in greased loaf pans and let rise till double. Bake in a hot oven 10 minutes and a moderate 50 more.

Makes 3 medium loaves.

KAFFEE KAKA (Coffee Cake) WITH VARIATIONS

1 c milk	1 T warm water
⅓ c shortening	2 beaten egg
⅓ c sugar	12-20 cardamon seeds or 1 T
1 t salt	almond extract (optional)
1 cake yeast	4-5 c flour

Pour the scalded milk over the next 3 ingredients. Add the yeast softened in the water. Add the eggs, cardamon, and 1 c of the flour. Let rise till light and bubbly. Add the rest of the flour. Knead until smooth. Let rise again till double in bulk. Put in greased pan and sprinkle with B. sugar and cinnamon. Let rise till double; bake in a hot oven 10 minutes and a moderate 30 more. Use this dough for:

KAFFEE KAKA

Buns.—Make in smooth, round shapes. Put a cherry or nut on the center. Brush with melted butter and sprinkle with sugar. Let rise on a greased pan till double in bulk. Bake in a hot oven about 10 minutes.

Semlor, or Shrove Tuesday, buns.—Shape dough into round buns. Place on a greased baking sheet, brush with beaten egg, and let rise till double in bulk. Bake in a hot oven about 10 minutes. Cool. Cut the top off and scoop a hole in each bun. Fill it with almond paste, replace the top, and dust with C. sugar. Commercial almond paste is the easiest to use, but you may make your own (Neopolitan Bread, p. 193). Omit flour.

Swedish tea braid.—Separate the dough into 3 parts. Mold these into long ropes and braid them. Pinch the ends together to form a circle. Glaze with 1 beaten egg mixed with 1 T water. Let rise on greased baking sheet till double in bulk. Bake 30 to 40 minutes in a hot oven. This is not as difficult as it sounds.

Swedish tea ring.—Roll dough out ½-inch thick. Brush with plenty of melted butter. Sprinkle with chopped, blanched almonds; cinnamon; sugar; and chopped raisins—if desired. Roll as for jelly roll. Put roll on a greased baking sheet, being careful to pinch all edges together to form a ring. With scissors, snip 1-inch sections all around the ring, but do not cut through to the bottom. Turn each section so that the fruit and nuts show. Let rise till double in bulk. Brush with beaten egg yolk mixed with water, and strew with more chopped almonds. Bake 30-45 minutes in a moderate oven. When you take this really beautiful —if a bread could be called that—ring from the oven, you'll know what the "baking thrill" is.

Makes 3 dozen buns or 1 large ring.

Mrs. Jessie Johnson Glans, Cleveland, Ohio

ORANGE RYE

4 c milk (sour for sour rye)	2 T finely pounded fennel seed (optional)
½ c shortening	½ cake yeast
1 T salt	1 T warm water
1 c dark corn syrup	12 c white flour
2 grated orange rinds	1½ c rye flour

Pour the scalded milk over the next 5 ingredients. Cool. Add the yeast softened in the water. Add the rye and ½ the white flour and blend all. Let rise till double in bulk (probably all night). Punch down and knead with the remaining white flour. Put in greased pans and let rise till double in bulk. Bake in a hot oven 10 minutes and a moderate 50 more.

Makes 4 large loaves.

LIMPE BREAD

2 c water	1 cake yeast
½ c B. sugar	1 T lukewarm water
2 t caraway seed	4 c white flour (about)
2 T shortening	2 t salt
1 t anise seed	2 c rye flour (about)

LIMPE BREAD

Boil the first 5 ingredients 5 minutes. Cool. Add yeast softened in warm water. Add the rest of the ingredients and knead well. Let rise till double in bulk. Punch down. Let rise again till double. Punch down and knead well. Put in greased loaf pans and let rise till double in bulk. Bake in a hot oven 10 minutes and a moderate 50 more.

This is a very famous Swedish bread that has a flavor like no other rye in the world. Watch a Swede's eyes light when you mention it.

Makes 2 large loaves.

Mrs. Jean Lindstrom Osmond, Cleveland, Ohio

SPISBRØD

¼ c corn meal	¼ cake yeast
½ c boiling water	1 T warm water
1 c warm water	2½ c rye flour
¼ t salt	graham flour for rolling

Pour the boiling water over the corn meal. Add the warm water and salt. Cool. Add the yeast dissolved in the water.

Add the rye flour, using more if necessary to form a stiff dough. Knead well on a board floured with graham flour. Roll very thin and cut in 10-inch rounds, with 2-inch holes in the middle. Prick all over with fork. Place these on a greased baking sheet for 1 hour. Bake in a moderate oven about 30 minutes.

Small amounts are given because not many people will want to have a great deal of this peculiar bread on hand. It will be like a rye cracker, very good with butter or cheese, but do not judge it by our standards of light bread.

Makes about 1 dozen.

SPISBRØD

SAFFRON BREAD

2 c milk	1 c sugar
1½ cakes yeast	1 beaten egg
1 t saffron	2½ T ground almonds
8-9 c flour	½ c chopped raisins
¾ c butter	¼ c chopped, candied peel

COATING

1 beaten egg	2½ T sugar
2 T chopped almonds	

Scald the milk and cool. Crumble in the yeast, the saffron, and half the flour. Let it rise double. Punch down. Add the butter and sugar creamed together, the egg, almonds, raisins, and peel. Add more flour if necessary to knead. Let rise again till double. Knead well. Braid into circles (see swedish tea braid, p. 215) and place on greased tins to rise. Cover with coating, and, when double in bulk, bake in a moderately hot oven about 45 minutes.

This will have a lovely yellow color from the saffron, and a mighty good taste.

Makes 2 circles.

SCOTLAND

The Land o' Cakes also does well by its breads. Some lover of the oat cake, one of Scotland's most interesting kinds of bread, has said, "Scotland has more reason to be proud of her oat cake than her short bread." Many people do not care for this rugged representative of the bread family, but one would indeed be hard to please if he couldn't find something to tempt him as he contemplates a well-filled Scotch tea table all covered with a great array of scones, muffins, pancakes, bannocks, and oat cakes, with the butter and the marmalade pot close by, and the teapot filled with tea guaranteed to take the Scotch mist out of one's bones.

In the olden days, barley was the usual flour used, but oatmeal gradually replaced it, and now, somewhat, wheaten flour is replacing the oats. Some Scotch people regret this, for they love their oats and even their barley.

Many of these breads are of the quick variety, but the Scotch know how to use yeast, and have for years. Their yeast is *barm,* which is really brewer's yeast made from the froth of fermented liquors. The origin of that word is rather interesting, by the way. It used to mean idle or bombastic talk. We know that in the 16th century there were at least four kinds of raised bread; the manchet or finest type; cheat bread, sometimes called trencher bread because it was used as a plate or trencher to hold the rest of the meal and then eaten; ravelled, a coarse bread containing all the bran; mashloch, a very coarse bread made of what was left after all of the fine parts of the flour had been sifted out. It is said that in the early days the Scotch commonly kneaded the bread with their feet, following the ancient Egyptian custom. True or not, it makes a good story.

The whole world should be as grateful to Scotland for giving it such a variety of good breads as the little child whose mother, in saying, "Give the bairn a piece," means a piece of bread.

BAPS *

4 c flour	1 cake yeast
1 t salt	1 t sugar
¼ c melted shortening	1 c milk

Mix the first 3. Mix the next 3, and combine the mixtures. Let rise 1 hour. Knead well. Make oval-shaped buns about 3 by 2 inches. Brush with milk. If "floury baps" are wanted, sift flour over the baps. Let rise on a greased baking sheet till double in bulk. Press the finger in the top of each before baking, to prevent blisters. Bake in a hot oven 15-20 minutes.

This is a word of unknown origin and meaning. But it is known that when these are served hot for breakfast, you'll have a mighty good meal.

Makes about 2 dozen.

BARLEY BANNOCKS *

1½ c barley flour	1 t sugar
1 t salt	1½ t melted shortening
½ t soda	⅓ c buttermilk or sour milk

Mix in order. Roll out on a floured board to ½-inch thickness. Cut into a round the size of a plate and bake on a hot, ungreased griddle over a slow fire until it is brown on the underside, about 10 minutes. Turn and brown on the other about 5 minutes.

The bannock, from the Gaelic *bonnach,* a cake, is usually applied to a large cake of this kind that is cut in pie-shaped pieces to serve. It should be baked on an ungreased griddle, or girdle as the Scots say, that is preheated and tested with a bit of flour dropped in. If it browns very quickly, it is too hot; if it browns slowly, go ahead with the baking. This word girdle comes from the Gaelic *greadeal,* a term applied to the ring of stones around a fire on which the earliest natives baked their little hearth cakes. Hence the idea of girdle. There are hundreds of kinds of bannocks, each one with some slight difference and many with some special-day significance. If they are made from such a mixture of flours as oat, corn, white, barley, they are mashlum bannocks. There's a St. Bride's bannock for the first of spring, the beltane for the first of summer, lamma for the first of fall, and hallowmas for the first of winter. In the highlands there is a salt bannock eaten on Hallowe'en to induce dreams that will foretell the future. No word must be spoken or any water drunk before the dream, or the spell would be broken. The cryin' bannock was made of oatmeal, cream, and sugar, and served to those assisting at a birth. The teethin' bannock, made of oatmeal, butter, and cream, with sometimes a ring in it, was given to a teething child to assist in that difficult process.

The bannock is difficult for moderns to bake properly because the usual gas stoves do not give the steady, controlled, slow heat that one gets from a coal range, or a stone in the ashes. Be sure to have a heavy griddle, or put an asbestos pad over the flame. It is possible to bake them in a slow oven, but this is not the way they are meant to be cooked.

Makes 1 bannock.

BARM BREAD

1 cake yeast	7 c flour
½ c lukewarm water	1 t each cinnamon, nut-
1 t sugar	meg, allspice
1½ c milk	1 t salt
1 c shortening	½ c currants
2 c B. sugar	1 c raisins
	½ c chopped citron

Mix the first 3 ingredients and let stand till bubbly. Scald the milk, add the shortening and sugar, and cool. Add this to the yeast mixture and add the rest in order. Mix well. Let rise till double in bulk. Knead. Put in greased loaf pans and let rise till double in bulk. Bake in a hot oven 10 minutes and a moderate 50-60 more.

This is a delicious fruit bread served in Scotland at Christmastime.

Originally the barm, or yeast, was made at home with hops or malt. If the dough was allowed to stand and get bacteria from the air, that was called virgin barm. If some old dough was used for a starter in the new bread, that was called Parisian barm. Barm itself means the foam from any fermented liquors and originally contained the idea of inane, or foolish, bombastic talk.

Selkirk bannock.—Make this recipe in flat round cakes, letting rise till double in bulk and baking about 40 minutes. This is a traditional Scottish Border recipe.

Makes 2 loaves.

CRUMPETS

4 beaten eggs	2 c flour
1 c milk	½ t salt
3 T sugar	

Mix to a batter. Drop on a greased griddle and brown on both sides over a slow fire.

These are not like the English crumpet, but more like Shrove Tuesday pancakes, that are eaten before Lent begins.

Makes about 1 dozen.

Mrs. Mary Watson McCall, Cleveland, Ohio

DEER HORNS (Doughnuts) *

½ c butter	4 beaten eggs
½ c sugar	2 c flour

Cream the butter and sugar. Add the eggs and flour. Chill. Roll thin, using extra flour if necessary. Cut in horn or crescent shapes and fry in hot lard as for doughnuts. Drain on brown paper and sprinkle with sugar.

For a variation add 1 grated lemon rind and 10 ground, blanched almonds.

These are rich and should be served the day they are made.

Makes about 3 dozen.

GINGERBREAD

2 c shortening	2 T caraway seed
1 c B. sugar	1 T allspice
6 eggs	1 t soda
4 c dark corn syrup	¼ c chopped, candied peel
8 c flour	2½ c chopped, blanched
2 T ginger	almonds

Cream the shortening and sugar. Add the eggs and beat well. Add the syrup. Add the sifted-together, dry ingredients, to which the fruit, nuts, and seed have been added. Pour into a greased shallow pan and bake in a moderate oven 1½ hours.

This is a spicy loaf that keeps well, is good for tea, but is not like our gingerbread except for the ginger.

Makes 4 loaves.

GINGERBREAD (Yeast)

1 c rye flour	1 T finely chopped orange
1¼ c white flour	peel
½ t salt	2 t ginger
¼ t caraway seed	2 T corn syrup
2 T chopped raisins	¾ c water
	¼ cake yeast
	½ T sugar

Mix all, adding last the yeast crumbled with the sugar and water. Let rise over night. In the morning, put in a greased loaf pan and let rise till double in bulk. Bake in a hot oven 10 minutes and a moderate 50 more.

This is a cheap Scotch gingerbread of the early days, but it has a good flavor and keeps well, so there's no reason why we shouldn't enjoy it.

Makes 1 loaf.

HOT CROSS BUNS *

1 cake yeast	1 c sugar
1 c lukewarm water	1 T cinnamon
6–8 c flour	1 T ginger
¾ c melted shortening	1 t nutmeg
3 beaten eggs	1 t cloves

Mix the yeast, water, and 1 c of the flour. Let rise till bubbly. Add the rest of the flour and the other ingredients in order. Let rise till double in bulk. Shape into round, flat buns. Brush with egg white and make crosses of little strips of dough on top of each bun. Let rise on a greased baking sheet till double in size. Bake in a hot oven about 20 minutes.

These are much like any hot cross bun without the fruit.

Makes about 5 dozen.

OAT CAKES *

4⅔ c fine, steel-cut oats
   or ground, rolled oats
1 t soda
2 t salt

6 T melted shortening
1 c water (about—butter-
   milk or whey may be
   substituted)

Mix all to a dough that will roll. Roll thin, using oatmeal on the board. Cut in plate-size cakes and bake on a greased pan in a hot oven about 5 minutes. Difficult, but possible.

These may be baked in pie-shaped pieces (farles), or they may be baked in either the round or quarter size on a griddle on top of the stove. They will keep well if packed in oatmeal in a tin box. Serve them with supper or as a cracker with cheese. The oat cake is a famous thing in Scotland, prized by some and called horse food by those who aren't appreciative of this delicacy. Originally, there were 4 implements used in the making of oat cakes: the spurtle or porridge stick used for stirring; the bannock sticker, or rolling pin, which made a crisscross pattern on the upper side; the spathe, a heart-shaped implement with a long handle, used for lifting the cake from the board to the girdle; and the banna rack or toaster. These used to be the Sunday bread of the cottager who had barley every other day. Makes about 2 dozen.

OATMEAL PANCAKES

1 c milk
2 c finely ground, rolled
   oats
2 beaten eggs
1 t sugar

½ t nutmeg
f.g. salt
½ t grated lemon rind

Scald the milk. Pour it over the oats. When cool add the rest in order. Bake on a greased griddle, over a slow fire, till it is brown on both sides.

These are served for tea, with butter, orange marmalade, and C. sugar.

They are not at all like our pancakes but like a soft tea cake. Makes about 1 dozen.

PLAIN PANCAKES

½ c milk	1¾ c flour
2 beaten eggs	1 t cream of tartar
¼ t salt	¼ t soda

Mix all to a stiff batter. Fry in small rounds on a greased griddle over a slow fire till brown on both sides. They may be varied with the addition of 1 grated lemon rind and 2 T crushed almond macaroon. Currant jelly is best with this kind.

SCOTCH PANCAKES

These are served hot or cold for tea with plenty of butter and marmalade. They are not like the American pancake at all, but like a "flannel" scone. Fine when you have cultivated the taste for them, as it is easy to do on a cold day in "The King's Arms" in a certain little town in Scotland.

Makes about 8.

Miss Roberta Abernethy, Columbus, Ohio

SCONES WITH VARIATIONS *

The word scone is properly pronounced "skonn" and comes from the Gaelic "sgonn," meaning shapeless mass. It is usually applied to a small, round or triangle-shaped cake baked on a griddle on top of the stove. We have included both girdle and modernized scone recipes for baking in the oven, for the results are more appetizing to people in this country, since it is more difficult to fry a good scone than to bake one.

GIRDLE (Griddle) SCONES WITH VARIATIONS

BASIC RECIPE *

4 c flour	1 t salt
1 t soda	1½ c buttermilk
1 t cream of tartar	4 T melted butter
	(optional)

GRIDDLE SCONES

Mix in order, to form a dough. Divide in 4 parts, making a round, flat cake of each part. Divide each part in 4 pie-shaped pieces. Flour all over and bake on a hot, ungreased griddle over a slow fire until well risen; then brown on the under-

DROP SCONES

side, about 10 minutes. Turn and brown on the other side, about 5 minutes. They also may be baked as a bannock in large rounds and cut at the table. These scones are very popular for breakfast. Makes 16 scones.

DROP SCONES

Use the above recipe, increasing the milk to 2 c and adding 1 beaten egg and 2 T sugar. They may be dropped directly on the griddle or dropped through muffin rings onto a griddle and baked till bubbly on top, then turned and browned on the other side.

MASHLUM SCONES

Use the basic recipe, substituting for 2 c of the white flour 2 c of any mixture of rolled oats, barley, rye, or whole-wheat flours. Follow the same baking directions.

POTATO SCONES

1 c leftover mashed potato	½ c flour

Mix to a paste that will roll very thin. Cut in small rounds and bake on an ungreased but floured griddle, over a slow fire, till they are brown on both sides. (These may also be baked in a moderate oven and turned once to brown.)

Serve them with plenty of butter and some salt. They must be eaten hot, and the best way is to stand at the cook's elbow while she bakes them and take them right from the griddle even at the expense of burning your fingers! Though some don't care for these, those who have cultivated the taste look forward to leftover mashed potatoes, for they mean scones.

Makes about 1 dozen.

Mr. Samuel Copeland Pritchard, Columbus, Ohio

SOUR SCONES

½ c rolled oats	¼ t soda
½ c buttermilk	1 t sugar
¼ c flour	1 t caraway, anise, or cardamon seed

Soak the oats in the buttermilk 3 days. Then add the rest. Roll ¼-inch thick and cut in triangles. Bake on a greased griddle until they are brown on both sides. These are sour, as the name implies, and are popular only with those who have cultivated the taste.

Makes 4 scones.

MODERN OVEN SCONES WITH VARIATIONS

2 c flour	⅓ c milk
3 t B.P.	2 beaten eggs
1 t salt	3 T melted shortening
1½ T sugar	

To the sifted-together, dry ingredients add the remaining ingredients in order. Mix lightly. Pat or roll ¼-inch thick. Cut squares, folding opposite corners together to make a triangle, or cut triangles. Brush with milk, or egg diluted with water, sprinkle with sugar, and bake on a greased pan in a hot oven about 15 minutes.

These are delicious, something like the American tea biscuit. They are good with tea, for breakfast, or with luncheon, especially a salad luncheon, and some people who are very fond of hot bread any time like them with dinner.

Cream scones.—Omit the sugar in the above recipe and substitute ⅓ c coffee cream for the milk. These are rich and good.

Fruit scones.—Add ½ c of any chopped, dried fruit, candied peel, or a mixture of both. This type is a special treat for tea.

Soda scones.—Use only 1 t B.P., substitute buttermilk or sour milk for the sweet milk, and add ½ t soda. This makes a good way to use sour milk and an excellent product. Sour cream may be used for a richer product—like the cream scone.

Spice scones.—Add 1 t of any kind of spice.

Toasted-oat scones.—Substitute ⅔ c rolled oats, that have been toasted in the oven, for the same amount of white flour. The toasting of the oats gives these a good, nutlike flavor.

Vanilla scones.—Add to the above recipe 1½ t vanilla. Do not serve this type of scone with a dinner as it is too much like cake.

Wheaten-meal scones.—Substitute 1 c whole-wheat flour for 1 c white flour. This appeals to those who do not care for the all-white-flour product.

Makes about 1 dozen.

Mr. Samuel Copeland Pritchard, Columbus, Ohio

---

* Adapted from McNeill, Marian, *The Scots Kitchen,* Blackie and Son, Ltd., London and Glasgow, with the permission of the publisher.

SWITZERLAND

This little country all hemmed in by other countries has borrowed as she pleased from their various cooking secrets and has blended them into a famous cuisine of her own. Swiss cooking is known and highly thought of all over the world; many a famous chef and many an excellent baker have come from the Swiss kitchen. Naturally we find the kuchen, the cruller, and the holiday bread that we have in all the countries surrounding Switzerland. But they're different. Try the New Year's bread and you'll agree.

CRULLERS

2 beaten egg yolks	2 T melted butter
1 stiffly beaten egg white	1⅔ c flour
2 T sugar	¼ t ground cardamon
2 T cream	(optional)
	⅔ T fruit juice or brandy

Fold the egg yolks into the white. Add the sugar, and blend. Add the rest in order. Chill overnight. Roll thin. Cut in diamond shapes. Make a slit in the middle and draw one end through the slit. Fry in deep fat as for doughnuts. Sprinkle with C. sugar, and serve.

Makes about 1 dozen.

CHRISTMAS BREAD

1 c milk	*Soak overnight:*
¼ c shortening	2 T brandy
¼ c sugar	½ t each cloves, cinnamon,
1 t salt	nutmeg
1 cake yeast	½ c sliced dried pears
1 T water	¼ c chopped citron
1 beaten egg	½ c chopped raisins
4 c flour	½ c chopped almonds
	½ c chopped green and
	red cherries
	½ t grated lemon rind

Scald the milk. Add the next 3 ingredients. Cool. Add the yeast softened in the water. Add the egg and flour. Let rise till double in bulk. Knead. Let rise again. Work in fruit mixture and mold into loaves. Put in greased loaf pans and let rise till double in bulk. Brush with melted butter. Bake in a hot oven 10 minutes and a moderate 50 more. Cool. Frost with a thin glaze made of C. sugar, hot water, and almond flavor mixed to a spreading consistency.

This is a great delicacy for anyone, but especially so for the Swiss lower classes, who look forward to the Christmas loaf as a child would to cake.

For a variation, replace 1 c white flour with 1 c rye.

Makes 1 large loaf.

NEW YEAR'S BREAD

1 c mashed potatoes	3 beaten eggs
½ c sugar	1 T salt
1 t salt	1½ c sugar
1 cake yeast	18-20 c flour
¼ c warm potato water	dried pears or other
4 c milk	dried fruit for decora-
1 c melted butter	tion (soaked till plump)

Mix the first 5 ingredients and let stand overnight. In the morning add the rest in order and knead well. Let rise till double in bulk. Knead again and shape into long loaves pointed at the ends. Put on a greased pan. Insert pear slivers all over the top of each loaf, brush the tops with cream, and sprinkle with sugar. Let rise till double in bulk, and bake in a hot oven 10 minutes and a moderate 50 more.

The real Swiss people use the pears, and this does give a wonderful flavor. Mrs. Fuchs says that this bread was always served in their home at New Year's Day. For a variation she uses:

NEW YEAR'S BREAD

Onion pie.—Fry 6 thinly sliced onions in lard until they are tender. Put in a greased pie pan lined with bread dough. Cover with a mixture of 1 T flour, 1 beaten egg, ½ c cream, and ½ c milk. Dot with butter. Let rise 1 hour and bake in a moderate oven about 50 minutes.

This is good for a supper.

Makes 6 large loaves.

Mrs. Anna Fuchs, Westerville, Ohio

POTATO COFFEE CAKE

1 c mashed potatoes	2 beaten eggs
1 c warm potato water	2 c milk
1 c sugar	1 T salt
½ c shortening	1 c sugar
1 cake yeast	½ c melted butter
10-12 c flour	½ t soda

Mix the first 5 ingredients and 1 c of the flour. Let stand 1 hour. Add the rest in order and let rise all night. In the morning, knead well and shape into coffee cakes in greased pans. Brush with cream and sprinkle generously with B. sugar and cinnamon. Let rise till double in bulk; bake in a hot oven 10 minutes and in a moderate about 30 minutes.

These are delicious coffee cakes that keep moist a long time. According to Mrs. Fuchs, when the dough is allowed to rise overnight it, "should be put in a large, white dishpan lined with waxed paper and covered with a red sweater." She says the best time to eat the coffee cake is just as it comes from the oven. Large pieces should be broken off and eaten with plenty of butter. Most people eat three before stopping!

Makes 4 large loaves.

Mrs. Anna Fuchs, Westerville, Ohio

THREE-IN-ONE

2 c milk	4 beaten eggs
⅔ c shortening	1 grated lemon rind
¼ c butter	1 cake yeast
1 c sugar	1 T water
1½ t salt	9 c flour

Scald the milk and add the next 4 ingredients. Cool. Add the rest in order, having softened the yeast in the water. Let rise all night. Knead and use in any or all of these 3 ways:

Rolls.—Shape in round buns. Let rise on a greased baking sheet till double in bulk. Brush lightly with beaten egg white and bake in a hot oven about 20 minutes.

Cinnamon rolls.—Roll dough in 1-inch-thick sheet. Sprinkle thickly with B. sugar, dots of butter, cinnamon, and raisins. Roll as for jelly roll. Cut in 1-inch pieces and stand close together in a greased, high-sided pan. Let rise till double in bulk. Bake in a hot oven 10 minutes and a moderate 20 more. These may be iced with C. sugar mixed with water to a spreading consistency.

Coffee cake.—Put in greased loaf pan and brush with cream. Sprinkle with B. sugar, cinnamon, and coconut. Let rise till double in bulk and bake in a hot oven 10 minutes and a moderate 20 more.

Makes 6 dozen rolls and 3 coffee cakes.

MISCELLANEOUS

ARGENTINA, CHINA, GREECE, HAWAII, PARAGUAY, PORTUGAL, WALES, OTHERS

In this section we have grouped the countries which do not have many characteristic breads, for which we were unable to find many representative recipes, or whose bread is so similar to that of other countries well represented here that it seemed unnecessary to repeat.

In the case of China, some doubt seems to exist as to whether the breads attributed to that country are really characteristic. Some people who travel in the Orient will come back with the story that there is no bread in China except imported European varieties, that the only Chinese equivalent of bread is rice. Others bring back actual recipes and insist that they are authentic and representative. Be that as it may, history tells us that a certain Chinese emperor taught his people the art of making bread way back in 2800 B.C. Maybe the art was lost, or maybe the steamed dough ball made of coarse flour and resembling a greasy doughnut that some call Chinese bread was the kind known to that emperor. Whatever the truth may be, we have included the recipes that people who have traveled in China assure us are authentic.

Hawaii cannot really be said to have had any characteristic bread until recently. Taro, known to the Hawaiians as *kalo,* has a very starchy root or corn that the early people cooked and pounded into a pasty substance they called *poi.* Poi is not like any bread we know, but was and is still used in Hawaii as a one and only dish for a meal—much as the orientals use rice.

Today, taro flour is made for commercial distribution by removing the fibrous exterior of the root of the taro plant and grinding the remaining, cooked portion into a very fine, gray, sandlike flour. This flour must be used with wheat flour as it is very high in starch and lacks glutenous qualities demanded for most baked goods. It gives to such things as waffles, pancakes, or muffins, a characteristic gray color and a definite, indescribable, but pleasant taste. It is not necessary to give any recipes; simply use any American recipe and substitute taro for part of the flour called for. In a recipe using 2 c of white flour, substitute ¼ to ⅓ c of taro for that amount of white flour.

Argentina

PAN PARAISO (Paradise Bread)

1 c milk, scalded	1 cake yeast
⅓ c shortening	¼ c warm water
¼ c sugar	1 beaten egg
½ t salt	3 c flour

Add the shortening, sugar, and salt to the milk. When this is cool, add the yeast, softened in the water, and the rest of the ingredients. Mix well. Let rise till double in bulk. Put the dough ½-inch thick in greased loaf pan. Cover with rows of thin apple slices (or any other fruit in season) and sprinkle with sugar and cinnamon and ¼ c cream beaten with 1 egg yolk. Let rise till double in bulk. Bake in hot oven 10 minutes and a moderate about 30 more.

This is a delicious sweet bread like the kuchen of Germany. Makes 1 large loaf.

Mrs. Russel Squire, Los Angeles, California

China

CORN-MEAL DATE CAKES

¾ c corn meal	1 c milk
1¼ c flour	1 beaten egg
5 t B.P.	2 T melted butter
½ t salt	1 c sliced dates
¼ c sugar	

Mix all in order. Put in greased covered can and steam 1½ hours.

This has a very good flavor and a moist texture. Makes 1 loaf.

STEAMED BISCUITS

2 c flour	1 T lard
2 t B.P.	⅓-½ c cold water
½ t salt	

Cut the lard into the sifted-together, dry ingredients. Add the water to make a soft dough. Roll ⅛-inch thick. Cut with biscuit cutter. Rub the biscuits with cooking oil (peanut oil is good) so that they will not stick, and place them in layers in the top of a double boiler. Fill the bottom of the boiler with boiling water and let the biscuits stand ready for steaming over this water for 10 minutes. Then put the boiler over the fire and steam for ¾ hour.

These are moist, will come apart easily, and are excellent with roast duck or pork.

Makes about 2 dozen.

Miss Katherine Bazore, University of Hawaii, Honolulu, T. H.

Greece

SWEET BREAD

½ c milk
¼ c butter
¼ c sugar
½ t salt

2 cakes yeast
2–3 c flour
2 beaten eggs

GREEK SWEET BREAD

Scald the milk; add the next 3 ingredients. Cool. Add the crumbled yeast cakes. Add the rest in order. Knead well, using more flour if necessary. Let rise till double in bulk. Knead again. Divide in 3 parts. Shape in 3 round loaves and place these on a greased baking sheet in the shape of a 3-petaled flower. Let rise 1 hour. Bake in a hot oven 10 minutes and a moderate 40 more. Cool. Frost with C. sugar mixed with water to spreading consistency. Decorate with nuts and candied fruit in flower shapes.

This is a most attractive loaf—good to look at and good to taste. Serve it for tea or a special breakfast, and don't cut it till it comes to the table.

Remember that, "where the loaves meet you'll find the kissing crust!"

Makes 1 loaf.

Paraguay

CHIPA

⅓ c melted shortening
1 beaten egg
⅓ c milk

1 t salt
⅓ c grated cheese
2 c corn meal
¼ t anise oil

Mix all to a stiff paste. With the hands, pat the loaf out on a slightly greased pan. Bake in a hot oven 10 minutes. Turn and bake again for 10 minutes.

This is a very odd-flavored, crumbly bread because of the peculiar combination of anise, cheese, and corn meal, but it has its admirers.

Makes 1 loaf.

Portugal

SWEET BREAD

3 c milk
2 T butter
2 t salt
1½ c sugar
3 beaten eggs

1 t lemon extract or
2 t vanilla
1½ cakes yeast
1 T warm water
10-12 c flour

Scald the milk. Add the butter, and cool. Add the rest in order, having softened the yeast in the water. Knead for 25 minutes. Let rise till double in bulk. Knead again. Put in greased loaf pans and let rise till double in bulk. Brush with beaten egg yolk. Bake in a hot oven 10 minutes and a moderate 40 more.

This is a very sweet bread that will stay fresh 4-5 days. It is fine for breakfast with plenty of good coffee.

Makes 3 medium loaves.

Dept. of Public Instruction, Division of Vocational Education,
Territory of Hawaii

Wales

BARA-BRYTH BREAD

3 cakes yeast	2 c raisins
¾ c warm water	2 c currants
1 T sugar	1 t cinnamon
2 T flour	½ t nutmeg
1½ t salt	¼ c finely chopped citron
4 T sugar	2 c potato water
1 T melted shortening	10-12 c flour

Mix the first 4 ingredients and let stand till bubbly. Add the rest in order and knead well. Let rise till double in bulk. Punch down and knead again. Put in greased loaf pans and let rise till double in bulk. Bake in a hot oven 10 minutes and a moderate 50-70 more.

This is the Welsh holiday loaf used in the Davis family for years.

Makes 3 loaves.

Mrs. J. B. Davis, Columbus, Ohio

Continental Pancakes

BASIC RECIPE

3 beaten eggs	½ c flour
2 T sugar	2 c milk
½ t salt	

CONTINENTAL PANCAKES

Mix all in order to a thin batter. Notice that there is no B.P. or shortening. This is like a thin omelet. Fry in large thin cakes on well-buttered, hot griddle until they are brown on both sides. Spread with any of the suggested fillings and roll. Serve hot as the main dish for luncheon or supper.

Since all continental pancakes are so much alike, and so unlike American, we give only this one standard recipe with a list of various fillings. Some countries have a special name, such as crêpes for France, eier kuchen for Germany, and blini for Russia, but, by and large, they are all the same.

FILLINGS

Almond.—Substitute ground, unblanched almonds for the cheese in the cheese filling below.

Applesauce.—Spread the cake with sweetened applesauce. Roll. Sprinkle with cinnamon and serve with syrup. They like this in Belgium.

Apricot.—Substitute cooked, mashed apricots or prunes for the cheese in the cheese filling below, and add ½ c ground, unblanched almonds. Popular in Hungary.

Cheese:

1 T melted butter	1 c cottage cheese
4 beaten egg yolks	2 T bread crumbs
1 c sour cream or sweet	2 t sugar

Mix all and spread. This is popular in Austria as a filling for the pancake they call palatschinken.

Cheese raisin.—Substitute raisins for half the cheese in the above.

Ham.—Substitute minced ham for the cheese in the cheese filling given above. Serve with sour cream.

Jelly.—Spread with butter and jelly, roll, and sprinkle with C. sugar.

Lard.—Fry pieces of salt pork, and pour the batter over them, turning the whole to brown. These are popular as crêpes au lard in France and are served at wakes, or before Hallowe'en, according to Mme. Alcide Brasseur, Lancaster, Ohio.

Raisin.—1 c raisins, soaked in milk till plump, and drained; 1 c sugar; and 1 t cinnamon. Mix, spread on the cakes, and roll.

BIBLIOGRAPHY

Apicius, Marcus Gabius, *Cookery and Dining in Imperial Rome.* Walter M. Hill, Chicago, Ill., 1936. (Dover reprint)

Austin, Thomas (Editor), *Two Fifteenth-Century Cookery Books.* Early English Text Society, Oxford University Press, 1888.

Cooper, Charles, *The English Table in History and Literature.* Sampson, Low, Marston Co., London, 1929.

Davis, J. R. Ainsworth, *Cooking through the Centuries.* J. M. Dent & Sons, London, 1931.

Encyclopedia Britannica.

Hackwood, F. W., *Good Cheer* (out of print). Sturgis and Walton, New York, N. Y., 1911.

Hazlitt, W. Carew. *Old Cookery Books and Ancient Cuisine.* Geo. J. Coombes, New York, N. Y., 1886.

La Wall, C. H., *History and Romance of Bread.* Philadelphia College of Pharmacy and Science, Talks of 1932.

McNeil, Blanche and Edna, *First Foods of America.* Suttonhouse, Los Angeles, Calif., 1936.

McNeill, F. Marian, *Scots Kitchen: Its Traditions and Lore.* Blackie and Sons, Glasgow, 1932.

Oxford Dictionary.

Shand, P. Morton, *Book of Food.* Alfred A. Knopf, New York, N. Y., 1928.

Spicer, Dorothy Gladys, "Bread Has Its Romance the World Over," *Baker's Weekly,* February 1933. American Trade Publishing Co., New York, N. Y.

White, Florence, *Good Things from England.* Jonathan Cape, London, 1932.

INDEX

A CATALOGUE OF
SELECTED DOVER BOOKS
IN ALL FIELDS OF INTEREST

A CATALOGUE OF SELECTED DOVER
BOOKS IN ALL FIELDS OF INTEREST

RACKHAM'S COLOR ILLUSTRATIONS FOR WAGNER'S RING. Rackham's finest mature work—all 64 full-color watercolors in a faithful and lush interpretation of the *Ring*. Full-sized plates on coated stock of the paintings used by opera companies for authentic staging of Wagner. Captions aid in following complete Ring cycle. Introduction. 64 illustrations plus vignettes. 72pp. 8⅝ x 11¼. 23779-6 Pa. $6.00

CONTEMPORARY POLISH POSTERS IN FULL COLOR, edited by Joseph Czestochowski. 46 full-color examples of brilliant school of Polish graphic design, selected from world's first museum (near Warsaw) dedicated to poster art. Posters on circuses, films, plays, concerts all show cosmopolitan influences, free imagination. Introduction. 48pp. 9⅜ x 12¼. 23780-X Pa. $6.00

GRAPHIC WORKS OF EDVARD MUNCH, Edvard Munch. 90 haunting, evocative prints by first major Expressionist artist and one of the greatest graphic artists of his time: *The Scream, Anxiety, Death Chamber, The Kiss, Madonna*, etc. Introduction by Alfred Werner. 90pp. 9 x 12. 23765-6 Pa. $5.00

THE GOLDEN AGE OF THE POSTER, Hayward and Blanche Cirker. 70 extraordinary posters in full colors, from Maitres de l'Affiche, Mucha, Lautrec, Bradley, Cheret, Beardsley, many others. Total of 78pp. 9⅜ x 12¼. 22753-7 Pa. $5.95

THE NOTEBOOKS OF LEONARDO DA VINCI, edited by J. P. Richter. Extracts from manuscripts reveal great genius; on painting, sculpture, anatomy, sciences, geography, etc. Both Italian and English. 186 ms. pages reproduced, plus 500 additional drawings, including studies for *Last Supper*, Sforza monument, etc. 860pp. 7⅞ x 10¾. (Available in U.S. only) 22572-0, 22573-9 Pa., Two-vol. set $15.90

THE CODEX NUTTALL, as first edited by Zelia Nuttall. Only inexpensive edition, in full color, of a pre-Columbian Mexican (Mixtec) book. 88 color plates show kings, gods, heroes, temples, sacrifices. New explanatory, historical introduction by Arthur G. Miller. 96pp. 11⅜ x 8½. (Available in U.S. only) 23168-2 Pa. $7.95

UNE SEMAINE DE BONTÉ, A SURREALISTIC NOVEL IN COLLAGE, Max Ernst. Masterpiece created out of 19th-century periodical illustrations, explores worlds of terror and surprise. Some consider this Ernst's greatest work. 208pp. 8⅛ x 11. 23252-2 Pa. $6.00

THE COMPLETE BOOK OF DOLL MAKING AND COLLECTING, Catherine Christopher. Instructions, patterns for dozens of dolls, from rag doll on up to elaborate, historically accurate figures. Mould faces, sew clothing, make doll houses, etc. Also collecting information. Many illustrations. 288pp. 6 x 9. 22066-4 Pa. $4.50

THE DAGUERREOTYPE IN AMERICA, Beaumont Newhall. Wonderful portraits, 1850's townscapes, landscapes; full text plus 104 photographs. The basic book. Enlarged 1976 edition. 272pp. 8¼ x 11¼. 23322-7 Pa. $7.95

CRAFTSMAN HOMES, Gustav Stickley. 296 architectural drawings, floor plans, and photographs illustrate 40 different kinds of "Mission-style" homes from The Craftsman (1901-16), voice of American style of simplicity and organic harmony. Thorough coverage of Craftsman idea in text and picture, now collector's item. 224pp. 8⅛ x 11. 23791-5 Pa. $6.00

PEWTER-WORKING: INSTRUCTIONS AND PROJECTS, Burl N. Osborn. & Gordon O. Wilber. Introduction to pewter-working for amateur craftsman. History and characteristics of pewter; tools, materials, step-by-step instructions. Photos, line drawings, diagrams. Total of 160pp. 7⅞ x 10¾. 23786-9 Pa. $3.50

THE GREAT CHICAGO FIRE, edited by David Lowe. 10 dramatic, eyewitness accounts of the 1871 disaster, including one of the aftermath and rebuilding, plus 70 contemporary photographs and illustrations of the ruins—courthouse, Palmer House, Great Central Depot, etc. Introduction by David Lowe. 87pp. 8¼ x 11. 23771-0 Pa. $4.00

SILHOUETTES: A PICTORIAL ARCHIVE OF VARIED ILLUSTRATIONS, edited by Carol Belanger Grafton. Over 600 silhouettes from the 18th to 20th centuries include profiles and full figures of men and women, children, birds and animals, groups and scenes, nature, ships, an alphabet. Dozens of uses for commercial artists and craftspeople. 144pp. 8⅜ x 11¼. 23781-8 Pa. $4.50

ANIMALS: 1,419 COPYRIGHT-FREE ILLUSTRATIONS OF MAMMALS, BIRDS, FISH, INSECTS, ETC., edited by Jim Harter. Clear wood engravings present, in extremely lifelike poses, over 1,000 species of animals. One of the most extensive copyright-free pictorial sourcebooks of its kind. Captions. Index. 284pp. 9 x 12. 23766-4 Pa. $8.95

INDIAN DESIGNS FROM ANCIENT ECUADOR, Frederick W. Shaffer. 282 original designs by pre-Columbian Indians of Ecuador (500-1500 A.D.). Designs include people, mammals, birds, reptiles, fish, plants, heads, geometric designs. Use as is or alter for advertising, textiles, leathercraft, etc. Introduction. 95pp. 8¾ x 11¼. 23764-8 Pa. $3.50

SZIGETI ON THE VIOLIN, Joseph Szigeti. Genial, loosely structured tour by premier violinist, featuring a pleasant mixture of reminiscenes, insights into great music and musicians, innumerable tips for practicing violinists. 385 musical passages. 256pp. 5⅝ x 8¼. 23763-X Pa. $4.00

"OSCAR" OF THE WALDORF'S COOKBOOK, Oscar Tschirky. Famous American chef reveals 3455 recipes that made Waldorf great; cream of French, German, American cooking, in all categories. Full instructions, easy home use. 1896 edition. 907pp. 6⅝ x 9⅜.   20790-0 Clothbd. $15.00

COOKING WITH BEER, Carole Fahy. Beer has as superb an effect on food as wine, and at fraction of cost. Over 250 recipes for appetizers, soups, main dishes, desserts, breads, etc. Index. 144pp. 5⅜ x 8½. (Available in U.S. only)   23661-7 Pa. $2.50

STEWS AND RAGOUTS, Kay Shaw Nelson. This international cookbook offers wide range of 108 recipes perfect for everyday, special occasions, meals-in-themselves, main dishes. Economical, nutritious, easy-to-prepare: goulash, Irish stew, boeuf bourguignon, etc. Index. 134pp. 5⅜ x 8½.
                                                                    23662-5 Pa. $2.50

DELICIOUS MAIN COURSE DISHES, Marian Tracy. Main courses are the most important part of any meal. These 200 nutritious, economical recipes from around the world make every meal a delight. "I . . . have found it so useful in my own household,"—N.Y. Times. Index. 219pp. 5⅜ x 8½.   23664-1 Pa. $3.00

FIVE ACRES AND INDEPENDENCE, Maurice G. Kains. Great back-to-the-land classic explains basics of self-sufficient farming: economics, plants, crops, animals, orchards, soils, land selection, host of other necessary things. Do not confuse with skimpy faddist literature; Kains was one of America's greatest agriculturalists. 95 illustrations. 397pp. 5⅜ x 8½.
                                                                    20974-1 Pa.$3.95

A PRACTICAL GUIDE FOR THE BEGINNING FARMER, Herbert Jacobs. Basic, extremely useful first book for anyone thinking about moving to the country and starting a farm. Simpler than Kains, with greater emphasis on country living in general. 246pp. 5⅜ x 8½.
                                                                    23675-7 Pa. $3.50

PAPERMAKING, Dard Hunter. Definitive book on the subject by the foremost authority in the field. Chapters dealing with every aspect of history of craft in every part of the world. Over 320 illustrations. 2nd, revised and enlarged (1947) edition. 672pp. 5⅜ x 8½.   23619-6 Pa. $7.95

THE ART DECO STYLE, edited by Theodore Menten. Furniture, jewelry, metalwork, ceramics, fabrics, lighting fixtures, interior decors, exteriors, graphics from pure French sources. Best sampling around. Over 400 photographs. 183pp. 8⅜ x 11¼.   22824-X Pa. $6.00

ACKERMANN'S COSTUME PLATES, Rudolph Ackermann. Selection of 96 plates from the Repository of Arts, best published source of costume for English fashion during the early 19th century. 12 plates also in color. Captions, glossary and introduction by editor Stella Blum. Total of 120pp. 8⅜ x 11¼.   23690-0 Pa. $4.50

GEOMETRY, RELATIVITY AND THE FOURTH DIMENSION, Rudolf Rucker. Exposition of fourth dimension, means of visualization, concepts of relativity as Flatland characters continue adventures. Popular, easily followed yet accurate, profound. 141 illustrations. 133pp. 5⅜ x 8½.
23400-2 Pa. $2.75

THE ORIGIN OF LIFE, A. I. Oparin. Modern classic in biochemistry, the first rigorous examination of possible evolution of life from nitrocarbon compounds. Non-technical, easily followed. Total of 295pp. 5⅜ x 8½.
60213-3 Pa. $4.00

PLANETS, STARS AND GALAXIES, A. E. Fanning. Comprehensive introductory survey: the sun, solar system, stars, galaxies, universe, cosmology; quasars, radio stars, etc. 24pp. of photographs. 189pp. 5⅜ x 8½. (Available in U.S. only)
21680-2 Pa. $3.75

THE THIRTEEN BOOKS OF EUCLID'S ELEMENTS, translated with introduction and commentary by Sir Thomas L. Heath. Definitive edition. Textual and linguistic notes, mathematical analysis, 2500 years of critical commentary. Do not confuse with abridged school editions. Total of 1414pp. 5⅜ x 8½.   60088-2, 60089-0, 60090-4 Pa., Three-vol. set $18.50

Prices subject to change without notice.

Available at your book dealer or write for free catalogue to Dept. GI, Dover Publications, Inc., 180 Varick St., N.Y., N.Y. 10014. Dover publishes more than 175 books each year on science, elementary and advanced mathematics, biology, music, art, literary history, social sciences and other areas.